Journey

of 1000 Miles

Hank DeBruin & Tanya McCready

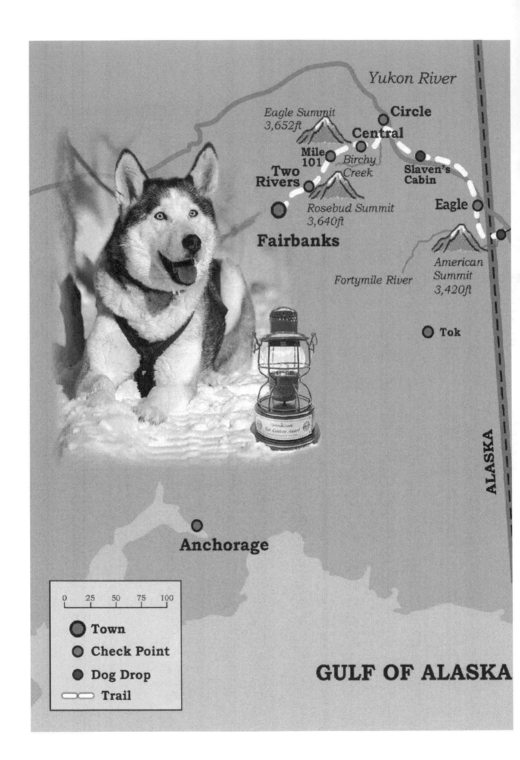

Fortymile

Dawson

King Solmon's Dome
4,049 ft

Scroggie
Creek

Stepping
Stone

Pelly
Crossing

McCabe
Creek

Carmacks

Braeburn

Whitehorse

NORTHWEST TERRITORY

YUKON TERRITORY

YUKON TERRITORY

YUKON TERRITORY

BRITISH COLUMBIA

CANADA

Reviews

Funny, heartwarming, page turner......This book is a MUST READ

This book is a MUST READ! It was a page turner and it warmed my heart. The story is so beautifully told and how Hank overcame his fears (on and off the ice / snow) & his doubts and overcame... I'm not quite the same after reading this book. It didn't just inspire me in an intellectual way. It made me see my world and what I'm capable of differently. I know I can overcome too. The book is also funny in parts! Funny and surprising and uplifting and sooooooo relatable. Wow.

—SunShine Daily - Amazon Review

Great Read about dogs doing what they were bred to do

Just finished reading Journey of 1000 Miles .....and loved it! I didn't want to put it down, and definitely didn't want it to end. The book makes you feel like you're actually part of the journey, in the sled with Hank, and you will be hard pressed to not fall in love with each of the Siberian Huskies pulling it. You can tell how much Hank and Tanya (and their entire team) not only love the dogs as a team, but know and respect them each as individuals. Easy to read, hard to put down.

—Karen F. - Amazon Review

Easy read – riveting!

This is a grassroots book, written from the heart. You will fall in love with the dogs, develop a huge respect for Hank and his team, and learn alot about how strong a connection can be between man and his dogs. I felt like I was on that dogseld!

—Betty Jo P. - Amazon Review

How Challenges are Overcome with Teamwork

Bought this book, could not put it down. The challenges faced throughout the book that were overcome with the teamwork at home and with the dogs. A beautiful journey thru beautiful country. Well written, enjoyable, easy read. Highly recommended.

—Denis P.- Amazon Review

Absolutely Inspiring

As the owner of a husky and a fan of anything husky related this book was an amazing read. I have always been in awe of dog sledding and the connections between a musher and his team. This book really makes you feel so many emotions and it's super hard to put down! Loved it!

—Amazon Review

Amazing Read for Any Dog Lover, A Magical Journey

Journey of a 1000 miles is a definite on my favourite reading list. It is an amazing read for any dog and adventure loving reader. The story takes you along with Hank and his dogs, on a magical journey as they prepare for and run the Yukon Quest. You feel like you are with them on the sled as his story unfolds and it gives the you a close first hand insight into the love and devotion and the special bond that mushers have for their dogs, and the challenges that they face day to day to survive and run the Yukon Quest, A journey of a 1000 miles. I highly recommend it.

—Jo B. - Amazon Review

Fabulous Read

If you have ever been curious about what it's like to travel the frozen north - in the depths of winter - by dogsled - this is the book for you. Hank and Tanya are able to put you in the seat with them as Hank and his team of loyal and determined dogs run the Yukon Quest dogsled race. It's a story of passion, dedication, perseverance, loyalty and love - for dogs, family and sport. The storytelling transports you to the race and you feel and experience the trials, tribulations, fears and successes along with the team. It is also a real reminder about the power of teams, leaders and the role of each individual in the success of the team. A delightful read!

—Amazon Review

Be ready for an amazing adventure right along with the team

From the comfort and warmth of my couch, I shivered, I cried, I laughed, I tensed up head to foot and I ultimately cheered, and cried again. Whether you are a dog lover, an adrenaline junky, an outdoor enthusiast, or just enjoy curling up on the couch with a good book, Journey of 1000 miles has something for you. An easy read, a page turner however you want to describe it, putting it down is tough to do. Thank you Hank and Tanya for taking me along on an adventure I could have never even imagined. I have added the Yukon to my travel bucket list. Seeing it in person is a definite must, after falling in love with it page by page. I look forward to future Winterdance stories from the trail.

—Sue Y. - Amazon Review

Wonderful Book

I absolutely loved every page of the Journey of 1,000 Miles! Filled with adventures, the book steals your heart from the first pages. Hank's simple and honest narration makes you feel as if you were with him every step of the journey. You can feel the excitement in the air at the start line. You can sense the dogs' need to RUN. The bear and the moose encounters, the beautiful Northern lights, the amazing night race... Even though the race is happening at -40C Yukon, one feels the warmth of Hanks love and care for the dogs, his wife Tanya, his family and the team.

—Irina T - Amazon Review

Incredible Adventure Story

I loved this book! It's an incredible story of adventure, tenacity, resilience, and teamwork. I couldn't put this book down. I highly recommend reading it especially during this time to get you away from the stresses of everyday life. Truly amazing!

—SRS - Amazon Review

Exciting and inspirational

Very inspirational book with an emphasis on teamwork, overcoming obstacles, and believing in yourself and your team. This book kept me up reading late at night and stepping away from the cares of today. Have already recommended it to friends and family.

—Jane R. - Amazon Review

A Fabulous Read

Reading this book was a complete joy. I was hooked from beginning to end. Learning not only about the dogs and Winterdance but also about the competition was fascinating. I became very invested in the dogs and their well-being and developed an even greater respect for Hank and Tanya and how the dogs and the dog's health and safety was their priority. I am looking forward with great anticipation to the next book.

—Lisa - Amazon Review

"I honestly could not put (the book) down once I started reading. This book hits all the emotions and sucks you in with its descriptive nature. I have never been dogsledding in my life, yet their writing style has you feeling like you are in the race yourself. The book is informative, yet very personal and candid. If you are a leader, there are many leadership implications that can be taken including, resiliency, dealing with adversity, teamwork and mind-set. This is a fascinating read and one that I am certain you will not regret purchasing."

—Jeremy A.

Dedication

This book is dedicated to the incredible huskies who not only made this journey a reality but are also some of our dearest friends in the world.

Lily, Strider, Aster, Hosta, Loretto, Jay, Andy, Gem, Maverick, Scully, Charlie, Zeus, Viper, Jed, Blitz and Howler.

Acknowledgements

There are so many people to thank who played a role in this project. They not only helped make the story possible but also helped create the book!

First, to the Yukon Quest family, made up of the mushers, officials, veterinarians, staff, villages and residents along the trail, volunteers, sponsors, and fans. You are the most incredible community we have ever been privileged to be part of. THANK YOU to all of you for making the Yukon Quest the incredible event that it is.

To our online and offline community who have sponsored and supported the team in so many ways to make our 2011 Yukon Quest journey possible, we couldn't have gotten to the start line without all of you. Thank you so much. Having all of you as part of these races brings so much more to the experience than it ever would be on our own.

Our staff make leaving for these races possible. Thank you to all of you for stepping up when Tanya and I are on the road. A special shout-out to Barb Bohlin, who looked after our children, our guides, our customers, and was also the first editor of this book. Thank you, Barb, for all you do for our family!

To Defining Moments and our ARC team, who helped edit and provide feedback on this book. Your time and efforts have added so much to this book. We are so grateful to all of you for your help.

Finally, a huge thank you to Richard Vladars for capturing the beautiful image on the front cover the first day of the race.

Table of Contents

1

Dark Spring

It was a perfect April day. The warm spring sun was glistening off the last remaining snowbanks, which were quickly melting. I always marvel at how +10°C in the spring feels like a summer heat wave after the long winter, yet +10° in the fall feels cold. Spring birds had already started returning, and they could be heard cheerfully singing in the forest that surrounds our home. Our huskies were also enjoying the lovely spring day, stretched out in the play yards soaking up the rays, for now content with being lazy.

Normally, this is one of my favourite times of year; sitting on the front porch of our log home with my wife Tanya chatting and just enjoying the slower pace of the beginning of spring. Our dogsled tours with our company Winterdance were over for the season and nothing urgent needed taking care of. Yet this year, I didn't see any of what I just described. This year, I sat on the porch in the sun yet in a very dark place. I couldn't see or find the joy in anything. All I could think of was the Iditarod trail, the race we'd dreamed of running for more than a decade, and how that dream, that race, had ended 300 miles short of the finish line. To be honest, that's all I'd been able to think of for over a month, since the phone call came in that ended our race.

I had failed. I had failed to finish and realize a dream Tanya and I had chased for over 12 years. I had failed my amazing dogs, my family, the friends and community members who supported this crazy dream of running the Iditarod. I didn't see or talk to anyone other than my immediate family. I had no desire to go to town, no desire to leave our property since we got home from Alaska over 4 weeks earlier. I just kept running the same questions through my head: "Where did I go wrong?" "What could I have done differently?" At first, when our race ended, I was angry—so angry! Angry at myself, at the race, at the race marshal, at life. Eventually, however, the anger subsided and turned into dejection and depression. Even splitting wood, which I find to be one of the best therapies in the world for working through anything that is troubling me, wasn't helping this year. I was completely lost as to how to move forward and didn't know if I wanted to anyway. What was the point?

Tanya had been sitting beside me for some time, lost in her own thoughts. She had been trying hard for the last month to cheer me up and make me feel better. Without looking at me, she quietly asked, "What about the Yukon Quest? Why don't you and the team run it next winter? So many people told us you and our dogs are more suited to that race anyway. We just didn't listen because Iditarod was always the dream. But now you are getting invitations from the Quest to come run their race, you and our team are welcome there. Why not take them up on the offer?"

I shook my head and said, "How? How can we possibly afford it?" The Iditarod had cost us over $50,000 to enter and run and, while we were blown away with how many folks had come forward and kindly sponsored a dog, some dog booties, a tank of fuel, etc., more than half the race costs had come from our pockets, and it had taken us several years to put aside the money.

"I've been running numbers and looking at what it would cost. The Quest wouldn't be as much as the Iditarod. We can do it. You need to enter the Yukon Quest and run and finish it next winter and show everyone it wasn't you, it wasn't our dogs, it was the Iditarod! We can do this!" Tanya said.

I didn't answer, but my mind was spinning. Could we make it work? Was it possible? I had no doubt our dogs could finish one of these races. I wanted so badly to prove it to all the naysayers and critics that had shown up online with all their "expertise" about my team and me since that day on the Yukon River, when a phone call from the race marshal ended our race. For the first time in over a month, I felt a stirring of hope, a feeling of excitement. Something to start focusing on and looking forward to again. Something to start dreaming and planning for. A second chance to chase a dream—just a slightly tweaked version of that dream.

I glanced at Tanya, who was smiling at me. "You can do this. I believe in you! They don't know you," she said. I smiled back. "You're sure we can make this work financially?"

"Absolutely" was her reply.

"The hell with Iditarod then," I said, "Yukon Quest, here we come!"

2

The Journey Begins

The Yukon Quest official sign-up day kicked off on August 4th, and Tanya had our entry all filled out and sent in that morning along with the $2,000 entry fee. We were listed as one of the first teams signed up, and the new goal was now very real. At the end of the day, there were 18 of us signed up to run the 2011 Yukon Quest. A nice incentive for signing up on the opening day included draws for free entry, a new parka, and 500 booties. It seemed like a wonderful omen when we heard our team had won the draw for the free entry.

While some of our friends in Alaska and the Yukon already had cool enough nighttime temperatures to start their training season, it would be at least another 3 to 4 weeks before it was cool enough here. It has to be 10°C or cooler for the dogs to start running to make sure they don't overheat. That gave me more time than I needed to dwell on what veteran dogs would be back on the team this year and what rookies would be trying out. We would start out training 24 dogs like we had for last year's

Iditarod and then drop that number to 20 by October before bringing that down to 16-18 by Christmas.

I had so many incredible dogs to choose from.

Max & Lily leading the raceteam on a training run in Haliburton

Veterans:

Lily – An easy choice. I have depended on her leadership skills almost as much as I did her dad Max's. A beautiful silver girl with a coat as soft as silk contrasted by her hard blue eyes that bore into whatever they are fixed on. Lily has a very strong personality to the point that no one messes with her, male or female. When we decided we wanted to have a litter of pups out of Lily, Tanya and I picked out several males in the kennel we thought would be potential matches. The first one was Murphy, my old leader. He went out into the yard, took one look at Lily, who was in full standing heat, and bolted straight back through the door into the kennel. Next up, brothers Phantom and Devil, who, while more than keen to try and woo Lily, also ended up running back inside the kennel, tails between their legs.

Letting Lily back inside the kennel, I watched her go up and down the kennel. She "chose" two dogs, brothers Ace and Harley. Harley was a bit leaner build and on my race team that year, so he got the nod. Eight weeks later, Lily gave birth to five puppies and Harley was the proud dad. Most of that litter are likely going to be on this team—Lily knew what she was doing.

Strider – Another easy choice. Strider came to us three years ago in need of a new home. He was supposed to be a Siberian, but his looks question his bloodlines. While he and I have some disagreements about the "correct" trail we should take at times, there is no doubt that he is an excellent leader with a huge heart. Strider is a ham and he loves affection and attention, almost to the point of being a show boater to get noticed. But when we have lots of people or distractions on the trail, I can definitely count on Strider to not get overwhelmed and to get us through it. Strider was one of my main leaders on the Iditarod trail last year and is one of the few dogs who can run in lead with Lily.

Aster and Hosta – I put these two brothers together because they are inseparable. They live together, run together, play together, and they are an incredible team. They are almost identical twins as well in appearance; except for a slight difference in the markings on their foreheads, most can't tell them apart. I often think of them as the guy on the work crew who you never ask to go get coffee. They are just serious, hardcore, no fuss dogs, fantastic workers. Both are a bit skittish with strangers, and both are built pretty leggy with the same grey colouring as their mom Lily. Hosta will run lead sometimes if I'm in a jam but will look at me and say, "all right, if I have too, but not for long."

Both are solid team dogs and happiest running side by side. While huskies usually love everyone, these two boys are my boys.

Loretto – An all-around great even-keeled girl. Loretto has no problem finishing someone else's supper; she's the biggest eater on the team. A tough, tough little girl, she will put up with no crap from her teammates, and, as such, can run with pretty much anyone anywhere in the team, making her an incredibly versatile dog to have on the team. Loretto will lead if needed but would rather not.

Jay – A stunning large wolf grey shade, fathered by one of my favourite original lead dogs Lazer, who taught me more about running dogs than any person or book. Jay has a superb attitude, tail always wagging, always ready to go. He has run with me in every race I have ever started and has never been dropped. He is one of those dogs you sometimes forget about because he is always giving his best and is always fine. Jay's also our indicator of temperatures getting too warm, as he is our heaviest coated dog. Jay is always happiest running in wheel position closest to me, and, with his size and strength, he makes a perfect wheel dog. Jay was also on our Iditarod team last year.

Andy – One of the easiest dogs to pick out on the team, with his brilliant red colouring and stunning blue eyes. Andy's first race was the Can-Am 30 with Tanya two years ago, and he did a great job for her. A solid working dog but also a clown when not working, Andy loves attention as much as Strider does. Andy got his name after Rick Swenson's (a 5-time Iditarod champion musher) great lead dog Andy. Andy was also on our Iditarod team last year and made himself a lot of fans with his colouring and outgoing personality.

Gem – A lovely little piebald coloured girl and Hosta's daughter, Gem (Gemmi as I call her) is as solid a dog as you could hope for. She has an amazing pace and stride. Even though she is smaller, she has no problem keeping up with the longer-legged dogs. Gem will run anywhere but lead and will work with anyone; she is the peacekeeper and peacemaker, always a happy girl, which makes her such a valuable team member when we have a lot of strong personalities. Gem is not real big on people, though; she enjoys being around them as long as they don't want to cuddle with her. Gem was on our Iditarod team last year.

Sapphire – Gem's sister, and also Hosta's daughter, Sapphire has a similar piebald colouring but her eyes are brilliant blue, hence her name. An incredibly driven dog, it is not hard to tell that Lily is her grandmother. She has a passion for running and work that equals her grandmother's. A crazy little ball of leaping fire is how I think of her. At five years of age, she is one of my main cheerleaders on the team. One of the last to be hooked up because she gets everyone else so wound up, she can always be counted on to pump up and motivate the team. Watching puppies as they grow, there are often signs of ones that you think will be leaders, and, in Sapphires case, she was the first one in her litter to do everything—jumping out of the box, fearlessly running down the aisle with all the adults barking at her and taking off, ripping around the play yards while her siblings Granite, Pearl, Gem, and Ebony hesitantly explored. We figured she would develop into a great leader, and she proved it her first year.

Maverick – At only two years of age, Maverick has already run the Iditarod and Can-Am trails. Tanya took him to the Can-Am 30 with her at a little over a year and, running in wheel, he did awesome and stole her heart. Maverick has lead potential for sure and is also a lover. He adores people and affection and, with his looks, he catches people's eyes fast. His bloodline ties into almost all the greatest lead dogs our kennel has been privileged to have, from Max, Lily, Gerdie, and RIP. Maverick has a funny habit when he comes off the truck of having to wave a paw at you before he is ready to jump out. He can be a bit of a clown, but then, he is only three this fall.

Charlie – Maverick's sister, these dogs were our Top Gun litter, so Charlie is actually a girl. Charlie was also on our Iditarod team last year and, while much smaller than her brother Maverick, is a personality people don't forget. Charlie is wild, crazy, brilliant, driven, and, at times, a bit of a flirt and trouble-maker! She loves having fun and getting everyone worked up but is intense like her grandmother Lily when running. I can see so many traits from all her grandparents in her. While I haven't tried Charlie in lead, I have no doubt she has lead potential.

Howler – Another Charlie, Maverick's litter mate, Howler's name is not Top Gun-themed, as she is so often, even as a puppy, howling to us. If you talk to her, she howls—supper time, she howls, time to run, she howls, if she is happy, she howls. It was just a given that her name would be howler. Howler enjoys people and attention but is quieter than Maverick and Charlie. I wouldn't go so far as to say she is shy, just more introverted and quiet personality wise, despite her howls. She is an absolute sweetheart. Howler trained for the Iditarod team last year but needed another year to grow up a bit more.

Jester – Another Top Gun pup, Jester is a hard-driving dog with a fun streak in him, as his name suggests, but a bit shyer than Maverick and Charlie around people. He has people he likes and doesn't like, and he doesn't seem to change his mind on them. Jester is a great wheel dog but is happy running any position, and on the whole gets along with everyone, so an easy male to work with. Not saying he is a pushover, though; if one of the other boys starts something, he is happy to hold his own. Charlie and Jester are best friends and live together.

Viper – The last Top Gun pup to try out for the team, Viper, is an almost identical twin to her sister Howler, like their dad Hosta. The only physical difference between the siblings is a tiny mark on their foreheads. Personality-wise, though, Viper is a lot more outgoing. Viper is happy to run in any position and with pretty much anyone, so is a versatile team member. She is a little crazier than Howler, too. I haven't tried Viper in lead yet, but with her love of adventure and life, I imagine she will make a great leader, too. Viper was on the Iditarod team last year.

Zeus - Zeus is the same age as the Top Gun litter, but he is a Lily-Harley son. Every pup in that litter has at least one of their mother's brilliant blue eyes. Zeus is as intense as his name suggests. The tallest of the pups in the two litters, he is leaner than Maverick but stands a bit higher. He is also a scrapper and enjoys a good brawl if he can antagonize someone into one. Maverick steers clear of him. Zeus is an incredible worker, though; you will never find his tug slack, and he lives to be in harness and travelling with a team. Despite his love of scrapping, when it is time to run, his energy becomes focused on the job at hand. He normally runs in wheel or very close to it so I can keep an eye on him. Zeus, while intense looking, is outgoing and loves attention. Zeus was on the Iditarod team last year.

Scully – Zeus's sister is named after Scully from the X-Files, one blue eye and one brown, and she is a dynamo. Boundless energy and personality, she is always on the move and interacting with other dogs. She and Charlie work well together and enjoy each other's company as well as being pretty much the same size. I have no doubt that Scully will also become a great leader, with her love of adventure and what is next. She is a fierce girl in her play and willing to jump into a fight, too, given the chance. Scully has a fun routine where she won't come out of the truck until she flips over on her back for a belly rub—then and only then, it is time to get to work.

Rookies that are trying out for the team this year include:

Jed, Blitz, and Miss Jane – They all trained last year for Iditarod but were just too young and lacking maturity to make last year's team. They are all amazing running dogs, so I'm excited to see what a year of growing up has done for them.

| *Jed* | *Blitz* | *Miss Jane* |

Nuisance, Abby, Strawberry, and Rosy – All siblings to Maverick, Charlie, Zeus, Scully, Howler, and Viper. All great dogs who live to run; again, last year they were just a little too immature to join the team, but a year has changed a lot for them.

| *Strawberry* | *Abby* | *Nuisance* |

The name that was not on the list was my incredible lead dog Max. At almost 13, the ceremonial start of Iditarod last March in Anchorage had been his final run on the raceteam. He would be staying home this winter and enjoying the more leisurely pace of introducing our guests from around the globe to the incredible world of dogsledding and the Canadian wilderness. Our guides who lead the 2-hour, half day and full day dogsled tours were over the moon to have him join them! How I would miss that dog on my team this year, though. Not only was he my best buddy but his intelligence, heart, drive, and passion had been an instrumental part of getting me and this team to the starting line of 1,000-mile races. He more than deserved semi-retirement, though I'm not sure he would see it that way. Given a choice, I have no doubt he would run up to the front of the team and, with stubborn determination, continue leading us. He would most certainly be with us in other ways, though, as most of the dogs on this team were his children and grandchildren.

September dawned warmer than I would have liked, and it wasn't until the early morning of the 11th that it finally cooled off enough overnight to head out on our first training run. We had five months until the start of the Yukon Quest. I ran 2 teams of 10 out of the kennel on the trail system on our home property. We could cover approximately 5 miles with the various routes and switchbacks I'd made over the years, more than enough for the dogs' first run after the summer off. After the first few training runs, they would come back into the kennel tired and diving for the water bowls, but give them a month, and this run would hardly even see them panting.

While we'd quickly outgrow the trails at the kennel, it was fun starting here, as it is so easy to harness all the dogs by just letting them loose in the yard and then hooking them to the ATV. Also, while Logan, Dustyn, and Michaela had started school the week before, Jessica, at 3 years old, was still home with us, and she loved helping to train the dogs. Great company on training runs was hard to turn down!

Jessica riding with Hank on a training run

We started a schedule of running 3 mornings a week, based on which days had the coolest temperatures. One group of 10 dogs would run, and then we'd quickly run the second group, assuming it hadn't gotten too warm already. Some days we would only get one team out and the other team would have to wait until the next cool morning, which was never popular.

The dogs this time of year get super pumped as they feel fall and cool weather in the air, which gets them to the point of hardly being able to contain their excitement. On frosty mornings, they would be howling at sun up in anticipation of snow and the adventures just ahead.

The teams were divided up to have veteran and rookie dogs on each team and, so far, there was not a single dog that didn't look like they belonged on this team. As we checked off training runs, the dogs got stronger and in better shape. October 8th saw our first frost, and the raceteam moved to their winter kennel, as the big wood furnace that heats the floors in the main kennel was about to be turned on. While we and the dogs love the heated kennel, dogs do grow slightly lighter winter coats in the warmth. With the raceteam sleeping outside during races, it was important for them to be used to that routine. While their outdoor kennel wasn't quite as warm as the indoor kennel, they had doghouses that were insulated and also had a deep bed of nice fresh straw for them to curl up into on cold nights. With two dogs sharing each bed, they were nice and cozy. During the day, though, if not training, most of them slept on the top of their doghouses.

October 12th welcomed a new member to our family as little Spot came into our lives. Her mom Pirate was a first time mom and wasn't too sure she wanted to be a mom at all. Getting herself all worked up in the delivery, she accidently injured Spot as she was born. At only a few minutes old, Spot was on her way to meet Dr. Laurie, our veterinarian. Dr. Laurie put in a couple of stitches to close up the small wounds but was more worried about any internal damage. Newborn puppies are so tiny and fragile, it doesn't take much for serious harm. We tried seeing if

Pirate would warm up to her new baby girl, but Pirate wanted no part of motherhood. It quickly became clear that we were now Spot's parents.

Michaela with baby Spot

Dr. Laurie told us the first day would be critical for her, and, if she made it through that, then the next 3 days, then the first week and reaching her first month birthday, we could feel she was out of the woods and on her way to thriving. We all committed to looking after her, and a nice box was made up with snuggly blankets and heating pads to keep her warm. Substitute mother's milk had to be warmed up and fed to her every 3-4 hours by a small syringe (we tried a tiny bottle but she wouldn't accept that). As we have 5 cats in the house who are monstrous in size compared to a newborn puppy, little Spot, tucked in her box, stayed in the cupboard under the kitchen sink to make sure she was safe from the felines. Our sons, who are huge Harry Potter fans, joked that Harry slept in a cupboard under the stairs and Spot slept in a cupboard under the sink! Tanya, meanwhile, mumbled one night at 3 a.m. as she got up to feed Spot that any thoughts she had for a fifth child were quickly disappearing with Spot's around-the-clock feeding schedule.

Mid October saw the team ready for more miles. With moose hunting season about to start, which lasts one week, we couldn't use our winter trails yet, so we loaded up the team and went to visit and train with our friends, the Goltons, about an hour east in Bancroft. They have an old rail trail behind their house and kennel that allowed for great training trails with tons of miles.

As we opened our home gate and pulled the truck into the yard, the raceteam heard it and started losing their minds. They knew it meant we would be running new trails today. The gate was closed and the doors to the inside kennel were opened so the raceteam could run through from their kennel to the front yard. They ripped through the back yard into the main kennel and out the front yard and were trying to jump into their beds on the truck, which took all of 7 seconds! There was no playing in the yard this morning. Everyone wanted to make sure they were on that truck ready for an adventure.

While going to Bancroft to train ends up taking most of the day, I enjoyed our runs there, not only for the new trails but it was also fun to visit with other mushers, which we didn't get to do very often. Ken Golton had been running dogs way longer than I had, and his teenage sons also trained and raced. Talk of past race adventures, training tips, dog food, gear, and all things mushing made the time after the run fly by as the dogs chilled, waiting for us to finish coffee and head home for supper.

On our third visit, though, we couldn't stay long. Friends Sue and Ed Yallop, who owned a restaurant called "That Place in Carnarvon," were kindly throwing a spaghetti dinner fundraiser for the team that night. All proceeds were being donated to help with the costs of running the Yukon Quest. While the dogs and I did a twenty-mile training run at the Goltons', Tanya, Barb, and the girls were cooking up tons of desserts for our guests coming to dinner. Our guide Jess was also busy grooming a grumpy Max, Snoopy, and Maverick to go meet our supporters that night. The three of them would have been far happier on the training run with me. Even little Spot got to come to the fundraiser, her first big outing. She slept in her box behind the bar with Ed while dinner was being served, and the kids took turns checking on her.

The raceteam got stronger and fitter, moving faster with every run and coming back less and less tired. Spot also thrived. As we rolled through November, Spot was growing like crazy and getting playful. All of us (2-legged and 4) were rejoicing in the first snowfall (not that it would stay on the ground yet), and with deer season behind us, it was time for the team to head to our touring trails 20 minutes north to continue their training. The home trails had done all they could for the team; it was time to start travelling bigger distances. I was excited for the change and to run different trails, and I was sure the dogs would be, too.

The fall so far had been quite wet, but the rain had eased up recently and trails were starting to dry out. Late fall normally brings its share of miserable weather as we dance between fall and winter; water holes skim over only to break up again, cold soaking rains turn into freezing rain and wet snow, muddy trails freeze into hard ruts and edges, and intense fog can roll in unexpectedly. Wildlife is also active as they, too, prepare for the oncoming winter.

The team loved being on our winter trails and heading across the hydro line through Algonquin Park. Some days, I would head out with the dogs on my own. Other times we'd take two ATVs and bring more dogs. On one run, we had an unexpected encounter. Dusk was closing in as we were headed home. From a clump of evergreens on the side of the trail, I heard a bawling sound and a second later, a yearling black bear bolted out of the treeline and seemed completely freaked out by us, crashing right into the team. It collided directly with Miss Jane, knocking her over, and the bear tripped and fell down, too. Both the bear and Miss Jane quickly jumped back to their feet, and the bear took off down the trail before veering off and crashing through the underbrush, still bawling. It was quickly out of sight. We were moving fast and fairly quietly, so perhaps it feared we were a pack of wolves. As much as the bear seemed freaked out, it freaked poor Miss Jane out even more. While she was happy to run with the touring teams, she no longer had any interest to train with the raceteam, and that would be her last run with the team. I tried to coax her several times, but, as soon as she realized it was the raceteam headed out, she wanted no part of it whatsoever!

As hard as it seems at the first of the fall to decide on the final team it gets easier as training continues. Sapphire sadly was dropped as a routine exam of a sore wrist led to an x-ray that showed she had a degenerative condition with her ankles. Training for and running marathon races was out for her so we could keep her safe and mobile into her old age. She was the hardest for me to cut from the team because it wasn't her decision…

Others were easier, Rosy decided she just wasn't enjoying longer runs that much. Nuisance was just too goofy and not mature enough. Abby and Strawberry were still too young mentally and were also too interested in fighting other ladies on the team, their personalities and Lily clashed big time.

We went out on another run in late November, when it hovered close to freezing. It had been fine when we headed out for the 40-mile run, with a brilliant sunset, but partway across the hydro line to Whitney, with dusk gone and dark settling in, fog started to roll in. It wasn't bad for a bit, but as we got close to the loop to start heading back home, it intensified to the point where it felt you could cut it with a knife. I could only see my back two dogs, Jay and Zeus. Lily and Strider were in lead and certainly knew the way home, but I found myself counting creeks as we ran to make sure we hadn't missed a turn. I stopped the team way more often than normal, much to their annoyance, to just walk up to make sure everyone was fine, as I couldn't see most of them at all. Blitz in particular, being jet black with no snow on the ground yet, scared me if he got loose. I moved him back in the team to keep a closer eye on him and to catch a glimpse of him more often as we hit light areas of fog.

Lily and Strider were incredible leaders, but I found myself really missing Max on this run. He had taken us through fog so many times before, and I had such total confidence in that dog to always bring us back to the truck or to the next checkpoint. Lily and Strider did awesome, though, and, as we hit another wet hole and made a hard turn, I knew they'd gotten us back to our home touring trails, and the truck was now only about 5 miles away. My confidence in Lily's and Strider's abilities grew even stronger that night.

Two mornings later found Tanya, the boys, Strider, Lily, Max, and I on our way to Toronto before the crack of dawn. Global Pet Foods had signed on as a sponsor of the raceteam and asked us to come help promote Woofstock, a dog expo, on the morning CP24 broadcast. We had lots of fun with the morning show hosts and even hooked up the team in the show's parking lot with a sled to show them what dogsledding was all about. The dogs put on an awesome show, even though there was only a few hundred feet to run before we ran into a parking lot barricade. The high pressure visit behind us, we had one more stop in Toronto before heading for home. Toronto is home to the world-famous Sick Kids Hospital, and Charlie had been honoured to be sponsored by one of the social workers from the hospital for the last two years. She had asked if there was any way we could stop at the hospital to meet with several kids—it was truly our pleasure! We all stayed outside the hospital in a little outdoor sitting area while kids took turns coming out to hug and love the dogs. The dogs were more than happy to meet with all the kids and make new friends.

The next morning, we woke up to a nice snowfall. Everything was coated in white like a Christmas card. While Tanya loves these mornings and grabs the camera, I think about how wet it is all going to be as it starts melting and falling off trees and how much work was ahead clearing and cleaning up from the weighted down trees and brush that will hang over or fall down onto the trails. But, on the plus side, we were headed back to Toronto to the Global Pets Woofstock booth, so I wouldn't have to deal with it that day. Mind you, with two trips to Toronto in two days, I would rather have been dealing with the wet snow!

14-year-old Cherokee was coming with us today. She was an ambassador for sure, falling in love with everyone she met and letting out the most delightful howls throughout the day. Cherokee came to us as a rescue 6 years before and fit in immediately. That said, every stray or rescue dog that came into our lives had always been an amazing dog, so maybe we read too much into it. They always seemed so grateful for a new home. Cherokee was one of the worst stories we ever had. Her owners moved away and called their neighbours who had a kennel of huskies and said, "We are moving and can't take our dog with us; she'll be tied to her doghouse if you want her." By the time our neighbours got over there, Cherokee's family had gone. They didn't even wait to see if the neighbours would take her.

Cherokee loved Woofstock. There were tons of dogs and people to meet, and the Global team discovered she loved their dehydrated liver treats. I'm sure she had a stomach-ache on the way home from all the treats she devoured that day. They even gave her a full bag to take home with her!

November 30th saw our first heavy snow fall, and I couldn't wait to pull out the sled and switch from ATV training to sled training. No engine, no heavy machine, and I could stand and be more a part of the team than I could just sitting on the ATV steering and helping with the engine. With no packed trail yet, the snowhook that acted as an anchor when I left the sled would not hold the team, so Logan came along with me for extra weight and to help hold the team when we needed to stop. I decided to take a team of 10. That's a lot of dogs for the first sled run of the season, and I admit I was full of nerves as I started hooking them up. Logan held out the leaders, and as soon as everyone was in harness and on the line, he let go of them and ran back to hop in the sled. What a 30-mile run we had! The dogs were childlike in their excitement to be on snow, and even though we were breaking trail in 12-18 inches of fresh snow for the whole run, they hardly slowed down. From the moment we left the truck, they were so happy. A quick stop for snacks for everyone had them all flopping over in the snow like children, rolling around in the fresh powder with sheer delight. As if the snow wasn't more than enough excitement, we also saw two moose in the distance and fresh wolf tracks. The dogs picked up their pace with the scent of the wolves and the sight of the moose, but the moose took off as soon as they heard us, and we never caught sight of the wolves. This run was as close to perfect as it gets—energy, attitude, trails, scenery, weather, everything simply aligned that day, and I was glad one of my children was with me to enjoy it, too.

The "near perfect" wasn't too last, as it often doesn't this time of year. The next day brought heavy rain and almost all our snow melted, so we decided to give everyone the day off rather than train in the mushy, cold mess. We were rewarded the next morning with another foot of snow on the ground, and everything looking Christmas card perfect again. Being December, I hoped it would last and we could stay on the sled and start breaking trails in for the touring teams.

The next several weeks saw winter indeed here to stay with more snow falling and our Winterdance dogsled tours starting for the season. We spent the days working on trails and the evenings into the night out training the raceteam. They were doing awesome, and I couldn't have been prouder of them and how they were becoming a team. Andy's desire to lead and his growing skills impressed me.

Training is about getting everyone in good shape, of course, but it is so much more than just physical conditioning. As we train, we are constantly switching dogs around, trying them in different positions and with different teammates to find out where they are happiest. A dog that might have had no interest in leading last year might be an awesome leader this year.

Forty- to fifty-mile training runs continued daily through mid December as I alternated which dogs were off each night— not that anyone ever wanted a night off! Tanya would tell me that those on their nights off would howl for a good chunk of the evening while we were gone.

On two nights in a row as we ran quietly, we heard two different wolf packs howling back and forth to each other a fair distance apart. You see, the dogs' ears perk up and listen with interest, but they keep moving at their normal pace quietly. If Cherokee were with us, she would happily have answered their howls!

The week before Christmas, the raceteam covered 300 miles. As I proudly said to Tanya, "I've never had a team like this before." Grinning, she said, "Gosh, I've never heard you say that before…" Snow was coming regularly, and the raceteam were constantly opening trails and loving it. Deep snow was not going to be a problem on the Yukon Quest trail at least. Wildlife was still abundant, too. One late afternoon we headed out breaking trail, and, as Lily and Strider rounded a corner, I saw a puff of snow like an explosion going off right in front of them. Lily and Strider both put on the brakes instantly out of surprise only to see a grouse take off unscathed. It had been staying warm, burrowed in the snow, until we annoyingly scared it off. Around 11 p.m. on that same run, the dogs' twitching ears and raised noses told me they'd caught the scent of something. Several minutes later, I started to notice a lot of fresh wolf tracks. The way it was snowing, they weren't far ahead of us. The dogs picked up their pace a bit, but we never saw them. Back at home, Spot continued to thrive and was now a 9-week-old puppy wrecking havoc on our Christmas tree.

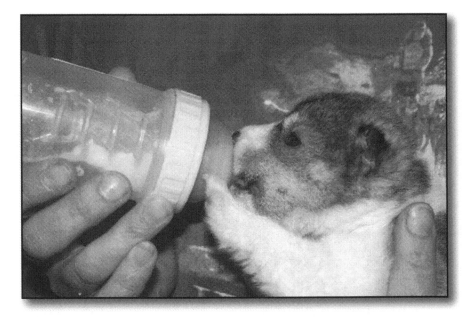

Spot enjoying her bottle

December 24th saw us out for a 75-mile training run and heading back home as dark set in for Christmas Eve. We had started out early that afternoon to be home in good time for Christmas Eve fun with the kids, but things don't always go as planned... We were about 20 miles out from the truck when, in a heartbeat, everything changed. From the side of the trail, I caught sight of something large moving fast towards us, and the next second, we had a moose jump into the team 6 dogs back from the leaders. I hadn't noticed it until the last second, and neither had the dogs. I think my headlamp blinded it as we approached and it stumbled into the team and then bolted in fear, running down the team towards me and the headlamp. I threw myself and the sled sideways and the moose went right over the handlebar and kept running. I jumped up and righted the sled as I set the snowhook all in one motion. Scanning the team with my headlamp as I did, my heart stopped to see Loretto lying in the snow, not moving. The rest of the team were all on their feet as much in shock at what had just happened as I was.

I ran up the line to her praying she wasn't hurt badly, or worse... A full-grown moose would weigh in around 1,200 lbs. If it had kicked her or stepped on her as it ran down the team...I couldn't let my mind go any further. I fell into the snow beside her, calling her name, but she didn't move. Then, with huge relief, I saw she was breathing. There was no sign of blood or any injury. Gently, I unsnapped her from the gangline and carried her back to the sled. Laying her down carefully, I rearranged the sledbag to make room for her to ride comfortably and tucked her inside with a blanket wrapped around her. She watched me, conscious now but still quiet and making no effort to move. I went back up and checked each dog, looking for any injuries, but everyone seemed fine and they were starting to lunge and howl to get moving again. I had no radio reception on this part of the trail to alert Tanya to what had happened, but, when I did, I checked Loretto before radioing and was thrilled to see her stretch inside the sledbag, looking stronger. I let Tanya know we had had a run-in with a moose and that was why we were running late.

Back at the truck, Loretto hopped out of the sledbag when I opened it up, but she was still unsteady on her feet. I put her in the cab with me and, as quickly as I could, loaded the rest of the dogs and the sled on the truck to head home for what was left of Christmas Eve with the kids. By the time we were back to the kennel, Loretto was looking much better but heavily favouring her front leg. I put her in the front of the kennel that night so I could keep a close eye on her. It was a Christmas Eve neither Tanya nor I will forget, and, while that encounter freaked me out, I was so grateful that all the dogs were home safe and sound. Ironically, we had written in our first book, *Iditarod Dreamer*, that we never had issues with moose on our trails, that it was a problem mushers in Alaska and the Yukon deal with. Needless to say, I had been proven wrong, and, as if to drive the point home, that was not to be our last moose encounter this winter.

3

A New Year

2011 rang in with the team sitting still. It became clear when we went for a short run after Christmas Day that, while the moose didn't injure any of the other dogs directly (other than Loretto), there were a lot of sore wrists and shoulders from our encounter. Giving them a few days off this close to heading to Michigan for a 300-mile race was not the plan by any means, but not allowing minor aches to heal would do us more harm in the long run.

After two days of rest, we let the team out into one of our large play yards to see how everyone was moving. Watching closely, I was relieved to see no sign of tenderness in any of the team as they ran and played with each other, other than Loretto. We would head out the next day for a short, fun run, just to be sure there were no lingering issues.

The next morning dawned gorgeous and cool with fresh snow having fallen overnight—a perfect day to hit the trails. After the morning dogsled tours were back at the trailhead and those dogs settled in for their noon siesta, the guides helped me hook up the raceteam. I was thankful for the help, as after having not run for several days, the dogs' excitement to get running was simply over the top. The first 5 miles they practically flew, with me doing my best to keep their pace in check with the drag mat. My 160 lbs. didn't have much of an effect on 800 lbs. of crazy dog power, though. One of our biggest downhills was ahead, and we hit crazy speeds going down it; the team hadn't run like this all year. Then I thought I saw moose tracks beside me. I watched and, sure enough, there were more, and they were fresh. There was enough snow this year that the moose were thankful for our trails. It made travelling for them easy and relatively safe, as they didn't have to trudge through deep snow, making them easy targets for predators. Fearing the moose wasn't that far ahead of us, I got firmer with the dogs and we slowed down a bit. As we followed the moose tracks, I kept hoping to see them veer off the trail, but no such luck so far. I pulled my snowhook loose from the holster and held it in my hand, ready to sink it the second I caught sight of the moose to keep distance between the team and it. While we were moving quickly, we also were moving silently, so the moose wouldn't hear us. The light wind was blowing in our direction, so it wouldn't smell us, either.

Maverick's ears twitched forward and he lifted his head slightly, sniffing hard. Seconds later, the whole team was doing the same. They had caught scent of something ahead and their pace instantly quickened. We were still following the moose tracks. As we rounded the next bend in the trail, I caught a glimpse of it; a large bull headed away from us. I jumped on the brake and, at the same time, slammed the snowhook into the ground. It didn't hold, and the team kept surging towards the moose. Maverick, who was running lead on this run with Scully, was hell bent on catching it. It almost seemed that after our last moose encounter, the team had a grudge against the giants and wanted to settle the score. They clearly didn't realize odds weren't in our favour in a fight against a bull moose with a full, magnificent rack of horns still on his head. The moose knew we were here now and started running away from us, and that just made the dogs even more frenzied to catch it—they sensed its fear. From the moose's point of view, I'm sure they saw a dogteam as a pack of wolves; other than humans, the only predator they have. We chased the moose, closing in on him for another few hundred metres as I urgently kept trying to get the snowhook to hold the team, but the brake wasn't doing anything at this point. Finally, I slammed it down again and it held. As fast as I could possibly move, I grabbed the snubline off the sled and tied it tight to a tree for more security to hold the team in case the snowhook popped free. That done, the dogs were screaming at me for stopping the moose hunt. I quickly radioed the trailhead that I could really use some help up here. No way on my own could I turn a team around that was this intent on moving towards the moose, and I didn't know what the moose would do next.

I didn't have to wait long for the answer. With the dogs stopped but making insane amounts of noise, the moose stopped, slowly turned to face us, and just stared at the crazy, screaming dogs. I grabbed the axe out of my sledbag and ran to the front of the team. The moose at this point was about 10 feet from me. It lowered its head and started pawing the ground and snorting, then started shaking its massive head and horns back and forth. This snapped me right back to my childhood on our farm, staring at one of our barnyard bulls as he did the same thing. Seconds after those actions, that barnyard bull had charged and sent me as a small boy flying over the fence. Our barnyard bull would have been small compared to this massive bull moose. In the distance, I caught the sound of a snowmobile coming our way. Seconds later, it was beside me with two of our guides. The moose got more agitated but also looked a bit less certain. The guides gunned the snowmobile engine hard and started moving the snowmobile towards it, waving their arms and the axe and screaming (on top of all the dogs screaming). The moose raised its head and stared at us for a second, and then wheeled around and started running down the trail again—away from the team. The snowmobile followed it from a distance until it finally decided to leave the trail. I untied the team and the snowmobile stayed in front of us for a while to make sure the moose didn't come back out on the trail. Thankfully, we didn't see it again. The guides turned back to go help with the afternoon tours, and the team and I continued on towards Algonquin Park. We would make sure to come back home a different way. I wasn't taking any chances of meeting up with him again.

While I was relieved and quickly developing a strong dislike for moose the way this winter was going, the team was clearly in a different mindset. They seemed quite disappointed in my having ruined their fun. Maverick had made it clear that he now hated moose and that it was his mission to hunt them. To my dismay, the rest of the team seemed to agree with him… On the plus side, the dogs were all doing awesome and we ended that run with all of them in great shape with no signs of any soreness left from our first moose encounter.

The next day, I took a camera with me for a 55-mile run, as we had been seeing so much wildlife. Naturally, that meant we didn't see a thing this run! While disappointing from a photography point of view, I was fine with a calm run for a change, although, as we passed what we began to call "moose alley," Maverick's nose and ears were twitching like mad.

My brother-in-law Ward was at our house when I got home. He had gone to every single race I had run and would be heading to Michigan with the team and me for the 300-mile Seney in three days. He was here early to help Tanya and the guides start working on the drop bags that would have to be shipped to the Yukon while we were in Michigan. Drop bags, for those of you not familiar, are grain sacks that hold everything the team and I would need on the 1,000-mile trail. They have the various checkpoints and my name written on the outside of the bags, and the Yukon Quest makes sure the bags are all at the correct checkpoint awaiting the team's arrival. Our drop bags would contain meat and kibble for the dogs, booties for their feet, food for me, socks, gloves, hand warmers (*tons* of hand warmers), replacement plastic runners for my sled, boot liners, and extra clothes. Getting everything ready for them and packing them was a huge job. The year before, getting them to Alaska had been an even bigger job!

Late the next afternoon, I headed out for a good long run with the team. A 14-hour camping run through the night was the plan, and I strapped a bale of straw on the top of the sled for the dogs' beds when we stopped for a break that night. The run went like clockwork and around 10 p.m. we came across a nice clearing to camp. I shook the straw out for the dogs and they settled into it pretty quickly as I started the cooker and filled it with snow. By the time I had their booties all off and checked everyone's feet, the snow had turned to steaming water and I added in the frozen hamburger. Ten minutes later, it had all thawed into a nice soup as I ladled it into the bowls with kibble. The dogs were all content, and, as I served them their meal, they all wolved it down. Before I even had all the bowls picked up, they were curled up, peacefully sleeping.

I pulled out my sleeping bag from the sled, a Cabela's -40°C bag that would easily keep me warm on this -25°C night, and I laid it out in the straw with the dogs. I found myself tossing and turning and drifting off only to wake up soon after chilled, despite the bag. Finally, I warmed up and fell into a good sleep like the dogs. When I woke, I realized I had slept 2 hours more than I had planned. I was also sweating I was so warm. Starting to roll over, I realized why. Scully had at some point wiggled into the sleeping bag with me and was asleep on my chest. Zeus had curled himself up around my head, neck, and shoulders. This was no one-way relationship we shared—they looked after me as much as I looked after them!

We all had breakfast and then packed up and were running again to watch the sunrise. It was one of those perfect days— beautiful trails, not too cold, sunny, and hardly a breath of wind. The dogs were enjoying the day as much as I was; no drama, no agenda, just run and enjoy the day. Too soon we were back at the truck. I took my time looking after the dogs, enjoying the peace and quiet and their contentedness. Today, we would be getting everything ready for the Seney. A quick run tomorrow, and we would be on our way early the next morning.

Ward and Tanya had things well in hand when I got back, and the rest of the day was spent putting foot powder in booties and wrapping them up and packaging meat into zip lock bags for snacks.

Near the end of a training run

The next morning, after the touring teams, guides, and guests were out on the trail, I hooked up the raceteam for a short 15-mile run. Today would just be fun for me and the dogs. It was another picture-perfect day with no wind, the sun shining with just a few white clouds in the sky and not cold. The dogs always sensed a fun run, maybe because I didn't pack the sled as heavy or I was more laid back. Whatever it was, they knew, and, as we harnessed them and put them on the line, the sled was literally bouncing as it was tied to the truck. The dogs were lunging so hard to head for a run.

We flew down the trails, me riding the drag mat to check their speed, but we just had a blast. We were about 5 miles from the trailhead when the dogs' ears all perked forward and they went into a run. My thought was, *not another moose…* I hadn't seen any tracks at all, but the dogs had sure picked up something that had them excited. As we came down a hill, my hand on my snowhook ready to sink it fast, I saw what had them excited. Tanya had snowmobiled out to surprise us and to get some pictures. It was one of those days you don't want to see end, but, as the sun started dipping below the treeline, it was time to get back to the kennel. While Ward would already have the truck all packed and ready to go other than me, the dogs, and the sled, there was always a few last-minute things to do, and we all needed a good sleep before hitting the road early the next morning. As we pulled into the trailhead, I couldn't help thinking that, while most of the dogs were the same as last year's team, I knew I had never taken a dogteam like this to the Seney before.

I couldn't wait.

Maverick & Lily in lead as we headed back to the trailhead as the sunset

4

The Magic Carpet Ride

Team fed and sleeping for the night, I headed to the house. One of my favourite scenes in my life is standing on our front porch on a winter's night, looking in the front door and seeing the welcoming warmth of a roaring fire in the fireplace, kids, Spot, and the cats ripping around, Tanya there in the middle of it all. Growing up with 10 siblings, life was always a beehive of activity, and, while four children is a lot less than 11, between the business, the kids, and all our animals, life was certainly never dull or quiet, and neither Tanya nor I would have it any other way. We love the crazy, busy, beautiful messiness of it all.

I opened the front door, and, as I stepped inside, was hit by the warmth from the fire, the sounds of the kids, and a smell that would make your mouth water even if you had just finished eating. Tanya, Barb (the amazing woman who came to work for us several years ago but now has become part of our family along with her husband Gunars), and the girls were in the middle of cooking and getting all my food ready to ship to Whitehorse in the drop bags. The aromas in the air alerted me to fresh baked apple pie, chocolate chip cookies, steak casserole, rice and mushrooms, lasagna, and more. While the dogs ate like kings and queens on the trail—so did I! For last year's Iditarod, Tanya and Barb had cooked and packed all kinds of amazing meals that sounded and smelled perfect when they prepared them. Then I pulled them out of drop bags, squished and frozen in zip lock bags. All I needed to do was drop the bags in my hot water I used to cook the dogs' food and enjoy. But, as I got more and more tired, it just seemed like too much work and things also didn't look near as appetizing frozen and smushed as they had when they came out of the oven steaming. As a result, I had dropped over 10 lbs. on the Iditarod trail last year. I ended up just eating things that I could open and pop in my mouth.

Barb helping Jessica add chocolate chips to my trailmix

So this year, Tanya had changed the plan, and, while there would be some meals in with my drop bag, there were going to be a lot more snacks that I could just grab and eat while we were running or while I was caring for the dogs. Trailmix is one of my favourites. Tanya makes a custom blend that I love—cashews, almonds, raisins, pumpkin seeds, dried cranberries, pineapple, and papaya, and then, to top it off, some M&M's and/or chocolate chips. Jessica and Michaela, who are 6 and 4 years old, adore helping make it, giggling as Tanya pours all the ingredients in a huge bowl and they get to dig in deep with both hands to mix it all up. M&M's in particular are too hard to resist sneaking a few to munch on. Then they help scoop it out into individual snack size Ziploc bags. Some of my other favourite snacks that Tanya packs are Christmas cake, chocolate bars, meat sticks, fruit cups, and fried bacon that our neighbour and friend Gunars takes on cooking and wrapping for me every year. Tanya usually also packs surprise treats in various checkpoint bags and lovely notes when she thinks I might need them.

My snack food ready to be packed for the trail

I don't know how anyone can do a 1,000 mile race without an incredible support team, and there were none better than mine.

We all enjoyed a great dinner and then crashed for a good night's sleep. At six a.m., we were up loading our bags in the truck and then letting the dogs out of the kennel. They always knew when it was a big race drive, and they were jumping around us like kids at Christmas in their excitement to get on the truck and get going. Our sons Logan and Dustyn, who are 10 and 8 years old, would also get to come on this adventure, which, in the dogs' mind, just made things even more fun. Dogs on the truck, goodbye hugs to Tanya, who still hadn't managed to get to come to a Seney, as she was once again going to be dealing with drop bags while we were gone. Ward jumped in the driver's seat, I in the passenger, and the boys in the back. With final waves, we headed down the driveway Michigan bound.

While last year, getting drop bags to Alaska had turned into a chapter in our last book called "Drop Bag Hell," this year, things seemed to be under control. We had more experience with how things needed to be packed and what we needed. Everything was pretty much done and in the freezer in the kennel. It would just be a matter of putting all the items in the bags the day they had to go to the trucking company, and they would be on their way. With no USA border crossings this year, there was a huge amount of last year's challenge out of the equation. The skid that everything would be packed in was built, insulation glued inside to keep the meat frozen in case the truck drove through warm weather, and waiting to be put on a truck and filled. The benefit from the Yukon Quest was that we could provide all our supplies for Dawson on the truck, so we were able to go from the two skids we used last year to one skid this year, which would cut our shipping cost in half.

Michaela, Dustyn, Ward and our friend Jim
helping pack dog food in drop bags

As we rolled toward Sault Ste. Marie, where we would cross the border into Michigan, my mind drifted back to the first Seney we went to in 2009. I remember Tanya, Ward, and the guides almost had to physically put me in the truck. I had come up with every reason I could possibly think of to not go that year after having signed up. At the time, the longest race I had run was 120 miles, so to jump to 300 seemed impossible. On top of that, it was organized and run by three multiple Iditarod finishers. The intimidation of looking like an idiot who knew nothing around people like that added to my grasping for any reason to back out. But, between Tanya, Ward, and the guides, all those reasons were scratched off the list one by one, and I finally had no other option than to admit I was scared that I didn't know enough or that I would fail. Not willing to admit that, we had loaded the gear and dogs, then, full of anxiety, I had hugged Tanya and the kids with Ward at the steering wheel and headed down the driveway.

Now I couldn't wait to get there. Being our third time there, it felt like home, and the Seney folks made it so—from Al Hardman, who organizes the race, and his best friend Charlie, who helps with logistics, to Jim O and Jim W, whose places are checkpoints on the race, to veterinarians Dr. Tom and Dr. Nick, to chef (and everyone's mother) Kathy and her husband Stu. These people were now some of my dearest friends. I learned more running that first race than any race I had or have run since. There are no crowds, no pressure, just amazing trails and people with so much wisdom wanting to share it and help you learn and grow as a musher. Every musher should have the pleasure and experience of the Seney.

As we crossed the border into Michigan, all of us, including the dogs, were in high spirits. This was the boys' first trip to the Seney, but they got to travel to Alaska and back last winter with Ward and me, so this was a small trip to make up for not being able to come with us this winter. The Yukon Quest trail was no place for children, and there would be few hotels or things to do. Tanya and Ward would spend much of the race driving from checkpoint to checkpoint and most of the time sleeping in the truck.

We were in Newberry by mid afternoon and checked into the hotel. We headed over to Al's to see everyone and leave our drop bags and look after our Vet check. Al's goal with the Seney was to run it as close to a 1,000-mile race as possible, from the pre-race routine to drop bags and rules. That is one of the reasons it is considered a qualifying race for both the Iditarod and the Yukon Quest. The dogs also knew where they were and greeted our Michigan friends with as much happiness to be back and see them all again as Ward and I felt. Dr. Tom and Dr. Nick had fun interacting with each of the dogs that they already knew so well. Other than shy Aster and Hosta, of course, they were my dogs, and other than Michaela, who could do anything with them, they tolerated other people only as much as they had to.

Pre-race routine completed without the stress and crowds of the big races, we headed back to Newberry for dinner with the boys and a night in the hotel, as well as the promised swim in the pool before bed.

Eight a.m. the next morning saw us back at Al's getting ready for the start, and at 10 a.m., we were on the trail headed to Fox River. The race did loops, and almost every leg was approximately 50 miles. Al's to Fox River, Fox River back to Al's. Al's to Jim O's, Jim O's to Jim W's, and than back to Jim O's and back to Al's. The weather was beautiful, around -10°C to -15°C, and the trails as ideal as they get, fresh snow but a firm pack. This was likely the first race I had ever run that I went into without the slightest bit nervous. We weren't here to prove anything, we were just here for a great 300-mile training run for the dogs and to have fun.

Tanya always reminds me that my mindset affects the dogs more than I often realize. She says she can be 1,000 miles away and looking at my spot tracker (if I have one) during a race, watching the speed the team is moving at, taking into account conditions and terrain, and know exactly what my mindset is. The dogs, like any team, be it your family, co-workers, employees, or a sports team, feed off the energy of their leader. Well, today the dogs were on fire, happy and joyful, and that is exactly how I felt—and we flew. I had never had a team travel trails like we did that day and continued to do for the next three days. I had given Ward an ETA for each checkpoint, and we hit every mark within a couple minutes one way or another. Mushers talk about magic carpet rides when everything just comes together with a team and a race; well, the 2011 Seney was one magic carpet ride for us.

While we were on the leg between Al's and Jim O's on day 2, Tanya put a post on Facebook: "Have I mentioned lately how much I HATE drop bags!!!! I need a fairy godmother or Harry Potter to 'magic' 2 skids to Whitehorse by Saturday. Plan A went up in smoke and flames today, wonder if Hank noticed??" The trucking company that was to take our skids to Edmonton to Lynden, the company that would take them to Whitehorse had called the morning the skids were to leave Haliburton to say the truck wasn't full enough, so they had delayed its departure by several days. This meant our skids wouldn't reach Edmonton in time to get on the truck to Whitehorse that only goes once a week. I had no way of knowing, of course, but while the dogs and I were having the time of our lives and the boys were being spoiled rotten by the Seney crew and fed like princes by Kathy, Tanya and our team at home were scrambling to come up with another way to get our drop bags to Edmonton.

Three hours later, a plan was in place. My friend Jeff managed to use his connections and account with another shipping company to get our skid on a truck the next day. It was still expected to reach Edmonton with 6-8 hours to spare before Lynden's truck left for Whitehorse. That afternoon and evening, Tanya, with "help" from the girls (Jessica tried to pack her favourite plush sea otter in the skid to give him a trip back to Alaska), the guides, Barb and Gunars, packed all the drop bags, loaded them in Gunar's truck with the skids, and our drop bags started their long journey. By the time Ward and I even knew there was an issue, they were almost to Manitoba.

We were the only purebred Siberian Husky team at the Seney that year, but when the race finished and times for each leg were added up, we were in first place! We all had had a wonderful time at the Seney with lots of time to visit, share stories from Iditarod 2010, and hear stories from Jim O's Yukon Quest. Jim was the first musher I had sat down with who had run the race, and I was grateful for all his advice and shared knowledge. Ward didn't exactly agree... When the team reached Dawson City on the Quest trail, it marked the halfway point in the race. The Quest rules allowed for handlers to take over the care of the dogs during the mandatory 36-hour rest, and mushers could leave their teams in their handlers' care. Ward had been excited to stay with the team in Dawson City at the campground across the Yukon River from the town. Al was kindly lending us his artic oven tent with the little wood stove so Ward would have a nice warm place to stay while the dogs would be under another shelter that Ward and Tanya would build for them, with tons of straw to snuggle in. Jim O's stories, though, had Ward seriously questioning what he had volunteered for. The stories got wilder by the minute with talk of winds that would blow tents away and -60°C nights and hoar frost that was so heavy you had to scrape it off everything. I think Jim took great pleasure in making Ward fret and stew over how big of an adventure his Dawson experience would be.

With bellies full from Kathy's huge end-of-race breakfast, there were hugs and kind wishes from everyone for the Quest ahead and words from Al and Dr. Tom that meant so much to me. They talked about how far the team and I had come in the three years they had known us, and we promised that we would be back next year. We all got in the truck and headed for Ontario. The only members of the team not content were Scully and Loretto, who didn't get to run. Dr. Tom had felt stiffness in both of their wrists still from the moose and felt it was better they sit the run out. The boys and Ward had taken them on lots of runs and played with them, but nothing compared in their minds to being on the trail.

As we crossed the border back into Canada and headed for home, I wasn't much company as I kept dozing off, but Ward was used to that after a race. He had likely put more miles on our truck than Tanya and I had, doing most of the driving to races and home as I caught up on sleep.

We pulled up our driveway just as dusk had turned to dark. All the touring dogs were home for the day and the guides were busy feeding and caring for them. As the raceteam hopped off the truck, chores paused to allow them to head back to their outdoor kennel. As I watched the raceteam rip through the kennel and pass all our other dogs, I wondered, as I often do when we return from a race, if they tell the other dogs stories of where they have been and what they have seen. With their tails all held high, I also wonder if the raceteam think they are better than the touring dogs or if the touring dogs see the raceteam as celebrities. Who knows in the dog world!

Tanya and the girls came down and, with chores done, we shared some stories from the race before the guides headed out for the evening. Our family headed to the house for dinner. While it was relaxing in one way to be home, stress was also starting to build. Six days from now, we would be leaving again, this time headed to the Yukon.

I turned in early, as the next day we had media coming first thing in the morning. Canada AM's Loren Christie was coming to the trail with a producer to film a segment on dogsledding and the team heading to the Yukon Quest. The raceteam would go up with me for the filming, but we would only go out and do a short 10-15 mile run just for them to stretch and have fun. We would run every day this week, but nothing crazy. My plan at the moment was no more than a 40-mile run. I wanted them content and a bit tired before we headed out for the long drive to the Yukon, but having just come off a 300-mile race, they also needed to not push themselves hard, either.

The next six days flew by. Loren and his Canada AM crew were a blast, and we had a lot of fun hosting them. The weather was great, and we ticked off awesome run after awesome run. Ward and I had come up with a list of everything that needed to be packed on the truck for the journey, and he was busy putting it all together. I was helping when not running or looking after dogs.

As we got closer to the departure day, I got more and more anxious about the Quest. It was called the Toughest Race on the Planet, after all. Then three days before we were to leave, I got up and went to find Tanya. She looked up as I walked in and asked if I'd slept well. I nodded and said I did. Looking at me, she said, "you look calmer this morning." I nodded again, saying, "I can't explain it, but I had a dream last night. Lazer was in it, and all

I know is the Quest is going to be fine." Tanya nodded. Lazer had been one of our first great lead dogs and taught me so much about travelling with dogs and leadership. We had lost him to old age a year ago, and we all still missed him.

On the 2nd last run I took the boys with me for an adventure, it was hard for both them and me for them not to be able to come with us this time. We all had lots of laughs and fun on that run as they rode together in the sled.

Logan and Dustyn on a night run with the team and I

Finally, the last day at home. One more 30-mile run for the dogs, and we would leave that evening. As we were headed back to the trailhead as the sun was setting, Tanya showed up to take some pictures of the team. We stayed out there a bit, the dogs content to roll in the snow, and just talked about the weeks ahead. I would be gone for close to four weeks, and the kids wouldn't be coming this time. It would be hard on all of us being apart that long. Tanya would fly up just in time for the start and fly back as soon as I finished. Thankfully, Barb and and another lady were staying with the kids and making sure everything in the office with the tour reservations went smoothly.

Sun having set, it was time to get back home. Ward would have the truck pretty much ready by now. As we ran the last 10 miles, my mind was thinking of the beauty of the trails I was on and how lucky I was, and also of what I could only imagine the team and I would experience and see before we were back on our home trails again.

That evening flew by and, still not ready to leave with last minute things, we decided to sleep for a few hours and pull out early in the morning. Ward and I also couldn't fit everything in the truck. Ward had done a great job trying, but I believed we still needed more dogfood. The arctic tent and the straw we had packed were taking up a lot of room. We finally compromised on the number of bags of dog food that we would take, and the doors closed and locked.

At 5 a.m. the next morning, the truck was in the yard and the dogs let out. Leaving at this time of day, they definitely knew this was special. We let them run around and play for 20 minutes before we started putting them on the truck. Everything was done, everything was packed, it was time…

I hugged Tanya and all the kids, with emotions running high. Tanya always smiled and waved as we left, but I also knew as soon as we were out of sight, tears would flow, and, I admit, my eyes always watered, too, as we left.

Loading up the dogs to head to the Yukon

The first day's drive went well. Having left early, we made a very long haul and reached Thunder Bay 21 hours after leaving. Five hours of sleep, and we were back on the road again with hopes of reaching Saskatchewan by the time we stopped that night. Tanya also had a long night, with Suzy going into labour and ending up with a c-section and 4 new babies being born.

That plan went up in a blizzard a few hours later. The snow was getting heavier and heavier as we approached Kenora and, when we pulled in, we found out the road was closed and we were stuck there for the foreseeable future. That turned out to be almost a day. We were both fit to be tied. We (because of me) had cut it close enough in timing to get to Whitehorse, so we sure couldn't afford losing a day in Kenora. At 3:30 a.m., they opened the road, and we were quickly heading west. It took two solid days just to get out of Ontario.

Thankfully, the drive that day was good, and, by the time we stopped, we had made Edmonton. We were still a little behind, but it was manageable. The dogs were all happy, having run so much the last ten days they were content to snooze and watch the scenery, hopping out every three hours for a washroom break, snack, and drink.

The next day, we hoped to get through much of BC up to Watson Lake. The day started out great and then a strange noise in the engine blew that plan up, too. We limped into Meyerthorpe Alberta on a Sunday with a blown belt and not a store open. We could *not* lose another day or two. Tanya put out a note on Facebook asking our fans for help. One of our former guides was a paramedic in a nearby town, and he called and found us a place to put the truck inside so we could work on it. Ward went around town quickly, and the owner of the local NAPA store showed up and offered to open his store so we could get a belt and hopefully back on the road that day. Everyone was so incredibly kind, and by that evening we were moving again. We didn't get far before we stopped for the night. There were long stretches between stops in that part of the world, and we needed some sleep. Tomorrow, though, would have to be our most aggressive road day yet—we had to be in Whitehorse, and we were still a 20-hour drive away. That didn't even account for the time needed to let the dogs out to stretch every couple of hours.

We were on the road by 5 a.m. again. This stretch of road, you *do not* want to drive at night. The road itself, with the mountains you climb, is challenging enough, but there is also a ton of wildlife, bison being the main concern. Luck was with us that day, though, and we had good driving conditions and no issues. At 6 a.m. (after many switches in driving between Ward and me) we saw the lights of Whitehorse come into view.

5

Whitehorse – Gateway to the North

On February 1, Ward and I finally pulled into Whitehorse. What a drive that had been! Insanely, the weather here was +6°C with a chance of showers, while back home in Ontario a blizzard was raging. Thankfully, we had pushed hard enough that the delays on the road had not put us too far behind. We had still arrived in time for all the required vet checks and meetings.

Christine was kindly waiting to meet us. She had worked for us for a season several winters ago and had moved to Whitehorse with her friend Casey, who had also guided with us. Casey was out of town for the winter, and he had generously offered up his cabin just outside Whitehorse for us to stay and train at. Christine drove us over there to get us settled. I loved the spot immediately! Casey had built the log cabin himself from trees on the property. It wasn't big, but it was all you needed for a place to sleep, stay warm, and eat. It was so peaceful that the dogs and I felt right at home.

We decided to go for a run the next morning to let the dogs stretch and blow off some energy after the long drive. Christine offered to go to show me the trails. She knew the area well, having worked and handled for mushers in the area. We all had a great sleep that night. The dogs seemed to know the drive was behind us and enjoyed spending a lot of time that evening stretching, playing, and enjoying the sights and smells of our temporary home. We could hear howls from kennels nearby that had them perking up their ears and noses trying to catch scents before sending back answering howls.

The next morning after the dogs had their breakfast, Christine arrived. We took the dogs off the truck and put them on the stakeout lines around the truck. Most of them had gained a couple of pounds on the drive with all the food and lack of running. As Ward and I got the sled, harnesses, and gangline off the truck, the dogs started going nuts. We were certainly making our presence in the area heard! The dogs were digging at the ground, jumping in the air, howling, barking, and lunging to get running. When they were all so excited, wrestling them into their harnesses was an effort in itself! Finally, everyone was on the line, and Christine hopped into the sled bag; the plan was for a 35-mile run.

I was thankful for a guide, as I had no idea where we were going, and with the energy in this team, they weren't going to be willing to stop for at least several miles. I found my hands shaking as I went to pull the knot to untie the snubline that was holding the sled fast to the truck. I asked Christine if she was ready for a crazy ride, and she grinned and nodded. I yanked the knot and we careened down the driveway at an insane speed with trees whipping by. Christine hollered that we needed to turn right when we reached the road, so I hollered to Lily and Strider in my firmest tone, "Gee! Gee, guys!" The last thing we needed was a broken sled two days before the start. Lily and Strider swung the team hard the second they reached the road, and we cleared the turn fine. I was starting to think we should have hooked up less dogs for this run. We zipped down the road, and Christine pointed that we needed to fork right up and over a snowbank to jump onto the trail. Again, I called, "Gee!" to Lily and Strider, and they hopped up the snowbank and led the team onto the trail. It always gave me such a sense of pride in these dogs when they performed like this, especially in front of someone who didn't know them well. Lily and Strider are both such incredible lead dogs.

A gorgeous day for a training run on Annie Lake

The trail was soft, so that, thankfully, slowed us down some as the dogs worked through the snow; not a bad thing at all. A short while later, we dropped down onto Annie Lake. The scenery was absolutely breathtaking, one of the prettiest spots I have ever had the pleasure of travelling through with a team of dogs. There was a trail that ran around the perimeter of the lake, and we jumped onto it. Christine pointed out a cabin at the far end of the Lake. She said it was Musher Hugh Neff's place, and that several mushers use these trails. As we cruised around the lake, the dogs started to calm down and settle into a comfortable pace. They were all so insanely happy, and everyone was running great. With the lake looped, we headed off onto another trail. For the next several hours, we travelled through gorgeous country, and both the dogs and I were in our element. No pressure, just out enjoying a gorgeous day travelling trails we had never been on. Too soon we were headed back to the cabin and truck. The "Meet the Mushers" event was on that night, and in a few hours, I would be sitting in a row of mushers as we met fans of the race and signed posters. We pulled up to the truck and Ward had bowls and water ready for the team. With silly, happy grins on all their faces, they lapped it up and gulped down their snacks. We unharnessed them and they contentedly jumped back into their beds on the truck. They knew where we were and seemed to know the adventure would start very shortly.

As the sun set, Ward and I got changed and drove into Whitehorse for the event. Even though we were early and it wouldn't start for almost 30 minutes, I couldn't believe the number of cars at the Centre. It would turn out to be a fun evening despite the huge crowd that came out to drink beer, laugh, and socialize with this year's Yukon Quest mushers. With the Quest taking turns, starting one year in Whitehorse and then the next year in Fairbanks, it had been two years since residents and race fans had been able to spend a night out with mushers while they were wide awake and excited (and nervous) for the adventure to come.

Getting back to the quietness of Casey's cabin, Ward and I enjoyed the rest of the night with a warm fire going and lanterns lit. Before turning in that night, I headed to the outhouse that had no door. The stars lit up the sky even brighter than they do back home. A hint of Northern Lights moved across the sky and I felt so at home. Not only was this the dogs' homeland, it also felt like mine—even though I had only been here once before in the winter and once in the summer. The spell of the Yukon, they call it. The land called to me, the people felt like long lost friends, everything about the place spoke to me and made me feel at home. If only my family was here with me, it would have been a perfect night. I wasn't alone with my thoughts, though, as Ward mused about moving here as well. No wonder the miners from a hundred years ago were caught up in the magic of the land along with the lure of gold.

I woke well rested and we quickly looked after the dogs. It was going to be a busy day; vet checks, meeting, and Tanya would fly in later today along with my friend Jeff and my nieces Michelle, Jamie, and Tiana and nephew Robbie who were coming to watch the start as well. We also had the opening banquet. We packed up our belongings from Casey's cabin and headed back into Whitehorse.

The dogs made friends as they usually did everywhere we went, and the vet check was no exception. Out of town teams are given some of the last spots, so most teams had already done their checks when we showed up for ours. Maverick, Charlie,

Scully, Strider, Andy, Howler, Zeus, Jay, Jed and Blitz… all made fast new buddies and we had several Quest vets, techs, and other volunteers ask if they could take pictures with the dogs. The "Top Gun" team, as they called us. While we wouldn't be the fastest, we would have lots of admirers. The dogs all passed their vet check easily with no concerns.

Next, we had a few errands to run before I had to be in meetings and Ward would go to the airport to pick up Tanya. The meetings (like any meeting for me) seemed to drag on forever. First the meeting with the race marshal and trailbreakers to update us on trail conditions, race rules, and anything else they felt we needed to know before the start, as well as meeting this year's veterinarians. The Canadian Rangers did all the trailbreaking and marking on the Canada side, and what a great bunch of folks! The race marshal Hans Oettli also seemed like a great guy and, as he had run the Quest with Siberians Huskies as well, we had a lot in common. We had a musher meeting with the musher reps for the Quest and then finally talks from some of the race organizers about media, how the start would work, and where trucks needed to go. Ward also had a meeting for handlers that dealt with rules of what the handlers could and could not do, what was required of them, and updates about the roads they would drive. Information on how to make sure they were prepared for the remoteness of where they would be driving with a list of extra supplies for the truck in case of breakdowns, including brake fluid, belts, fuel, oil, flares, etc., and survival supplies like candles, blankets, food and water.

I always find the starts incredibly stressful. So many people who want to talk and interact with both me and the dogs.

Meetings, routines, crowds…just so many things that aren't part of our life. Being an introvert, it puts me out of my comfort zone, to say the least. Add to that all the anxiety around the race itself, and it is easy to let worry and emotions get away from you. I totally understand that the races need all these events to help make money. They also give the fans a chance to be part of the race and get to meet their favourite mushers. While it will never be my favourite part, I always do my best to try to connect with anyone who wants to, as they love the race as much as we do. Without the sponsors and fans, there would be no race to run!

We checked into our hotel that would be home for the next two nights. Casey's cabin would have been just fine with me in the middle of nowhere, but it was easier being in town for the events and last-minute errands. The High-Country Hotel, with a three-story Mountie carving in front of it, was an official sponsor of the race and where we stayed. The dogs, yet again, quickly made new friends. Ward, with his ability to make friends as easily as the dogs, just increased our list of new acquaintances, from the front desk manager to race volunteers and organizers. The dogs wouldn't get to run today with everything happening, but they were content with all the goings on and new people they were meeting.

I finished up my meetings finally and headed to our hotel room to find Tanya. While it had only been eight days since I had seen her, we aren't apart for long very often, and having her there just made everything better. I would feel a lot less stressed about all the little details, which, at the moment, were completely overwhelming. So much had been thrown at us in the musher's meeting—overflow, summits, jumble ice, starting procedures, and the list went on and on.

The banquet would start that night at 6 p.m., so we had a couple of hours to look after the dogs and get ready. The nice thing with long distance mushing banquets is that there is no need to get ready at all. While some guests would be dressed up, going in your normal everyday clothes was the norm—my kind of event! Turned out, as we headed to the conference centre 20 steps out the door of the hotel, the Quest banquet was even more laid back than the Iditarod banquet and less than half the size. Mushers all had reserved tables, and Tanya, Ward, and I made our way through friends and fans to find our table near the front of the room. My nieces and nephew and friend Jeff were also at our table, so between all of us, our table was already full.

Our table of friends and family at the 2011 Yukon Quest opening banquet.

There were two large screens set up, one on each side of the stage, that were showing slides from past races. I glanced up at one of the screens at one point and found myself rocked. I nudged Tanya sitting beside me and nodded towards the screen. Staring down at us was Lazer; although, it couldn't have been Lazer, as he had never run the Quest. I looked back at Tanya questioningly. She shook her head, saying, "I never sent them a picture of him, and that isn't one of our pictures anyway." I had never nor have I since met another dog that had Lazer's unique markings, but here was a dog that was his absolute twin staring down at us. A coincidence? Considering my dream two weeks ago, it was hard for me to think that it was…

A delicious dinner behind us, it was time for the serious part of the evening—the drawing of the starting order for Saturday. One by one, mushers went to the stage to draw their bib number. As I lined up beside the stage, nerves kicked into high gear, mainly because several mushers before me were taking the chance to thank their sponsors, talk to their fans, and entertain the crowd. I hated being in front of a crowd at all, let alone speaking. My words would be very short and sweet.

My turn. I drew the chip out and handed it to the race marshal, who announced I would be going out in 19th place. They also presented me officially with the cheque for winning the entry fee and the free box of booties. I had won a very nice bonus. I was fine with that starting position, not going out near the first, not at the back; a good number. In one sentence, I quickly thanked my sponsors, the volunteers, and my family, and I was off the stage.

The rest of the evening was full of laughter and stories as mushers visited and swapped tales. Friends and fans listened intently to the tales being told as alcohol flowed. Not a late-night party, though, as we all had dogs to care for, and the race start was only 36 hours away. We all needed a good night's sleep.

Banquet over, Tanya, Ward and I jumped in the truck and drove over to the nearby Walmart parking lot. The High Country Hotel parking lot was jammed full of vehicles, so there was no place to safely let the dogs out. Walmart parking lots are great, especially late at night/early morning when the store is closed. The dogs jumped off the truck quickly. This was the first they had seen Tanya, and they were as happy to have her with us as I was. They all gobbled down their dinner as Tanya went to each one to talk to them and give them love. After some stretches and rubs, though, they were waiting to get back into their beds quicker than normal. It was like they knew they needed a good rest.

The next morning dawned beautiful, sunny, and cool with no wind. This day would disappear in the blink of an eye, so staying on schedule was going to be vital to make sure everything got accomplished and ready for tomorrow. First item on the agenda after getting the dogs and us breakfast was to head out for a run. We drove out to Casey's again, my friend Jeff coming with us. The dogs started howling as we turned down Casey's road. They knew they were going for a run! They charged off the truck as we pulled the sled down and got everything ready to go. More hands today made harnessing and getting ready faster, which was a good thing considering the dogs' craziness to get moving. Tanya hopped in my sled to come with us and, like we did two days ago, we shot off from the truck and down the driveway. I hollered a hard "gee!" but there was really no need. Lily and Strider knew the trail now and would take us the same way we went the other day whether I told them to or not. The dogs were just as happy and wound up today as the last run, but I wasn't nervous now, knowing the trail, so they ran with more ease. Tanya brought her camera and, as we circled Annie Lake, she took some photos to share with our community. It was hard to put the beauty, peace, and solitude we felt out there on that run into a photo. We passed Hugh Neff's kennel again and got a rousing howl of welcome from his dogs. Our guy's ears perked forward and their tails went up a bit, but other than a glance in the other dog's direction, they kept moving by quietly.

Annie Lake, Yukon training run.
One of my favourite pictures ever of our team.

Tanya asked me how I was doing with the start being tomorrow. I was honest and said, "beyond anxious!" She laughed and asked, "What section are you most afraid of and why?" I thought for a minute as the dogs turned another bend in the trail on the lake and said, "After the start, my biggest fear is that 200-mile stretch of trail to Dawson. I'm worried about being able to bring everything that we need to go that long a distance." Tanya nodded in front of me, saying, "Well, others do it every year, and at least we can be in the checkpoints, so we'll figure it out together when the time comes." She was right, no sense worrying about a section of trail that I wouldn't get to for at least 3-4 days. I have found that to be an invaluable lesson while running the trails or doing anything large. While you always have your overall goal in front of you, your focus needs to be on today, this hour, just as far as you can see, or even just the next tree that you can see when things get bad. You can always travel one more kilometre or to the next tree. Just breaking things down until your mind goes, "well, we can certainly at least get that far." And then just keep repeating that—that is how you travel 1,000 miles.

Back at the truck after our short 6-mile run, the dogs all flopped out in the sun, enjoying the day as much as we were. We were all pretty relaxed, so the dogs were, too. While Tanya, the dogs, and I had been out running, Ward and Jeff had pulled apart the truck to organize what we would need for that night and the next day and figuring out what supplies we still needed to purchase before the start. I showed Tanya Casey's cabin, and she agreed it would be wonderful to have a cabin like that somewhere remote. I smiled, loving how we were always on the same page and had the same dreams and goals. As much as I wanted to stay here for the day and enjoy the peace and quiet of the wilderness, it was time to head back to Whitehorse and start getting ready for the next day. All the bins from the truck needed to come inside, and my sled would also come into the hotel to be carefully packed for tomorrow.

Ward and Strider - best friends

Dogs back on the truck, we made our way to Whitehorse. We hauled everything into one room, including the sled, to dry off. Ward headed off to do some shopping while Tanya and I started packing. Jeff showed up and, with tools in hand, kindly went over my sled tightening the bolts and checking over the mechanics of the sled to make sure everything was in good shape and that there would be no problems.

Now the fun began—trying to fit everything that I thought I needed into the sledbag. They say rookies pack everything but the kitchen sink in their sleds. I wasn't a 1,000-mile rookie anymore, but I had a feeling my sled would be just as full as it was on last years Iditarod's trail. After a fun, relaxed dinner, the packing had to get finalized. The list was endless; how many bags of booties, how many bags of kibble, and emergency kibble… In went the sleeping bag, axe, snowshoes, cooker, bowls, booties, more kibble, extra socks, and a change of long johns, just in case I got wet, stuffed up in the front of the sled. I added the first aid kit, medicine bag, fuel, repair kit, dog coats, dog blankets, and my wind suit, leaving room for frozen meat to be added in the morning. Then the small stuff was tucked into the inside pocket of the sled bag and small top pocket that I could easily get to without opening the main zipper and bag. Not to be forgotten were cable cutters, hand warmers, my snacks, more booties, batteries, and headlamps. Sledbag bulging at the seams, we tried to zip it up and, unsurprisingly, we couldn't. I decided to leave a couple of the dog blankets behind. With three of us leveraging the zipper, we got it closed. Now for my gear. We pulled out those bins, and I went through all my arctic clothing. My niece Michelle was helping us, and we dressed her up in all my gear. She couldn't believe how heavy it all was and was sweating buckets in moments!

Everything I would wear the next day was packed in one bin, and we loaded the truck with just what we would need for that day. Ward and Tanya would come back to the hotel and pack up everything else once I was on the trail. Then they would head to Braeburn to meet up with the team and me.

Everything done and last-minute items purchased, it was time to try and get a good night's sleep. While we were busy, it was easy not to focus on the start, but as everyone said goodnight and headed to their own rooms, my mind started focusing on the fact that in 12 hours, we would be getting ready for the start— nerves kicked in big time. We drove to Walmart to let the dogs out again, and they were all happy and bouncing around. I had no doubt they knew tomorrow was the big day. I also still wasn't totally sure which 14 dogs I was taking. I was hoping the final vet check tomorrow would help me decide.

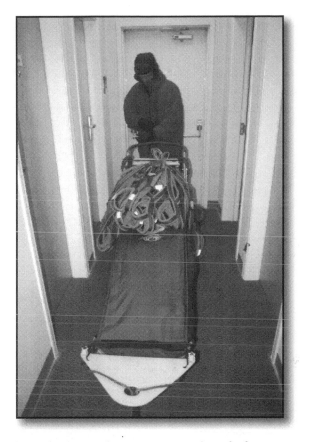

Sled packed inside the High Country Hotel ready for tomorrow's start

I tossed and turned for a while once I got into bed but finally managed to fall asleep and didn't wake until the alarm went off the next morning. The second I woke up, my mind was in full gear and I instantly felt ill from anxiety over the day ahead. Once we were on the trail it would be fine, but the next 5 hours would be torture, with my mind entertaining everything that could possibly go wrong. Tanya looked at me and said, "no breakfast I take it?" I grunted my response. Another quick drive to Walmart to let the dogs stretch and have breakfast (their stomachs didn't seem to be bothering them) and we were back at the High Country doing final packing and changing. Tanya had washed all my clothes, so I put on two layers of fresh under armour with my fleece overtop of that. I wouldn't put on the rest of my gear until we were 30 minutes from the start; no sense sweating at this point and then getting cold.

It was time to go. We drove the short distance to the starting line parking lot, and there were already dog trucks and trailers. Everywhere there were mushers, fans, volunteers, and hundreds of ramped up, excited dogs. Volunteers directed us to our parking spot as everything was organized in the order each team would leave the starting line. The next two hours would be hell. Freaking out inside, I did my best to look calm as photographers, fans, friends, mushers, vets, officials, and volunteers came up to meet the dogs, visit, and ask questions. The vets went over all the dogs again, checking ID tags and microchips and doing a quick physical. Loretto's wrist, we all agreed, was still slightly stiff from the moose over a month ago, so that meant, as unhappy as she would be about this, she would be staying with Tanya and Ward and not heading out on the trail with me. That meant Blitz was on the team—God help me. Blitz was so lighthearted and goofy. He still acts like a puppy and, at times, that can wear on me and the patience of the senior dogs on the team.

I wouldn't want to guess how many pictures the dogs had taken of them that 45 minutes they were out, but we decided it was time for them to go on the truck to chill for a bit away from all their fans. The sled was out of the truck by now and tied off to the front. We pulled the coolers out of the truck and packed all the frozen meat that the team would eat this run. There was no way another ounce of anything was going to fit into that sled bag. The three of us managed to get it zippered shut, and the bags of booties that we would put on the dogs before the start lay on top, ready. It was time to get my gear on. Tanya helped me with my big red Cabella's suit that we had stuffed in the inner liner in the sled bag. At -9°C and sunny, I wouldn't need to wear that layer to stay warm today.

Ward and I at the start, he has handled for me at every race I have run

All around us, dog teams were getting hooked up. Some were already going to the starting line, and the energy and excitement had ramped up 1,000 times. Our dogs were howling to get off the truck, so we obliged. Harnesses were all put on and then their booties. With Tanya, Ward, and Christine there helping, it went pretty quickly. It would take me much, much longer to do it on my own over the next 1,000 miles.

Twenty minutes until our starting time. Tanya grabbed my race bib and helped me snap it on. Freaking out doesn't come close to how I felt at that moment. It was time to put the dogs on the line. One by one, as quickly as we could, we put them in their spots. Lil and Strider would lead out, followed by Aster and Hosta, then Maverick and Scully, Jed and Blitz, Jester and Charlie, Andy and Viper, and in wheel Zeus and Jay. Loretto was furious at me. I felt horrible leaving her behind, but it was for her own good, not that she would ever agree... Howler was the other dog being left behind and while also not happy she wasn't looking at me the way Loretto was at least and should would enjoy the TLC from Tanya and Ward.

Tanya and I putting booties on the dogs as we get ready for the start

Fifteen minutes until the start, and the dogs were all hooked up, jumping, howling, lunging and screaming to get moving. We were as ready as we were ever going to be. Volunteers were patiently waiting beside dogs ready to help us to the starting line when we gave the word. More volunteers approached, motioning that it was our turn to start moving. With every second, the dogs' excitement grew as they watched other teams moving. I nodded to Ward, who was up at the front of the team ready to lead Strider and Lily to the start. He hollered at all the volunteers to be ready (it was the only way to be heard over the noise of all the dogs). I reached over to pull the knot loose that held the sled, and hence, the team, to the truck. That rope was drawn insanely tight to hold back the force of 700 lbs. of crazy husky. I glanced at Tanya, and she nodded standing right beside me. She put all her weight on the brake of the sled. I jerked hard on the rope; it only budged a bit. I pulled with all my strength, and the knot let go. We lunged ahead as the dogs got to finally move forward with their efforts. We moved quickly, though the volunteers checked the pace by pulling as hard as they could backwards on the gangline with the leashes they had attached to it. Tanya eased off the brake as my full weight and hers shifted to the drag mat to slow the team's march to the line. There were three teams lined up to go out in front of us, so we had eight minutes before we would be on the trail.

I *love* having a crazy dog team that is so passionate about what they are going to do. I wouldn't have it any other way, but at times like this, it is a lot to handle and attempt to control. *Three…two… one.* Another team was gone, and we moved up a bit closer to the start line. Lots of well-wishers came to shake hands and pat me on the back while we waited, but the dogs were focused on one thing, and that was getting out on that trail and running. Another team left the starting line. We were right alongside the building now where fans weren't allowed, so it was a little less crowded, but I could see there were fans lined up on both sides down the snowfence for as far as I could see. Another team left. Now we were the next ones to go into the chute. The volunteers had their hands full with our guys, but they did a great job holding them back. I could hear the announcer now and the cheers from the crowd as they cheered on Ken Anderson. And then he was gone, and Ward motioned to the volunteers. Our team started running as fast as the humans would let them, passing under the starting gate. These dogs all knew the drill. The sled came to an abrupt halt with the help of strong volunteers grabbing the stanchions as they braced themselves on their knees in the snow for maximum leverage against the dogs' strength.

Someone kindly offered to stand on my brake, and I went up to pat, talk to, and look each dog in the eye to connect with them. Their eyes showed their crazed need to *run*. Fans were cheering, and the announcer was saying we were from Haliburton, Ontario—the team that had travelled the furthest for the race—and he was talking about our beautiful Siberian Huskies. I didn't hear a word. At 30 seconds, I was back at my sled. The race marshal Hans shook my hand, wishing me a good run, and I hugged Tanya as we both whispered "I love you" and "be careful!" While she saw my part of the race as the most dangerous, I was equally worried about all the miles and remote roads Ward and her would be travelling to meet up with the team at checkpoints. They had one heck of an adventure ahead of them, too, and would travel more miles than the team and I would.

Ten…nine…

Tanya went up the team petting each dog and waving the handlers away. Ward stayed at the front with Lily and Strider. I reached down and, with hands shaking, pulled my two snow hooks out of the snow and sunk them into their holders on the sled. Adrenaline was raging through my body, as what I was about to unleash, I wouldn't be able to control for several miles.

Five…four…three…two…one…

The volunteers released my sled, and the team exploded out of the starting gate, jubilant to finally be able to run to their hearts' content. Tanya reached out her hand as we sped by, and I gave her a high five as we passed. My nerves were gone now. What was forgotten was forgotten, no second guessing could change anything now. This was the moment we had been training five months for. Let the adventure begin!

We are off! With Lily and Strider leading we charge out of the starting chute

6

Gold Rush Trail

In seconds, we were past the crowd cheering at the starting line, and another difference quickly came to light between the Quest and the Iditarod. In the Iditarod, on the first day you pass spectators and fans all along the trail. In the Quest, other than the bridge up the trail a couple of miles where folks gathered to cheer on mushers and snap photos, the trail was quiet and peaceful. My nieces and nephew along with Christine's friend Robert, who captured the cover photo, were waiting and waving at the bridge as we passed.

It was just shy of 100 miles to Braeburn, our first checkpoint, and I planned to break this run into two sections, stopping to let the dogs rest for five hours around the 45-mile mark. But for now, there was certainly no resting. The dogs were running on pure adrenaline and wouldn't be ready to listen to me for a few miles. They were so happy, tails out, heads and ears straight forward, just enjoying running and travelling together as a team.

Most of this run was on rivers and lakes with some land trails in between—The Klondike trail. So incredible that, over 100 years ago, dog teams were running these same trails hauling mail, goods, and people to Dawson City and back. Part of what I love about running dogs is the incredible connection you feel to the past.

Day 1 on the Yukon River leaving Whitehorse

Close to an hour after we left the starting line, I started to notice ears swivelling back in my direction occasionally. The dogs were starting to remember I was back there and were interested in what I was doing and planning. They would listen to me now; it was easier to control their pace to what I wanted it to be. The afternoon was spent enjoying a gorgeous winter's day running north. Occasionally, a team would pass us or we would pass a team pulled over to snack. I would stop every two hours religiously to give the dogs a snack. Thin frozen strips of steak were their favourite quick snack.

People often ask me, what is the most important thing I carry with me on a distance race? It is hard to choose, as any single thing I pack in the sled has vital importance to the success of the journey, but without a doubt, one of the tools I depend on the most is my watch. I use it to know when it is time for us to stop for a snack but also to gauge the distance we have travelled. After having spent years behind a dog team, you have a good feel for the speed your dogs are running at. The difference between a 5 mph tough breaking-trail kind of run versus a 20 mph chase after a deer or rabbit is easy to tell, but distance mushers can even tell the difference between 10 and 8 mph. When you know how fast your dogs are travelling, you can use your watch to quickly work out how many miles you have travelled and how long it is going to take you to get to the next checkpoint. Who said I wouldn't use math and physics after school?

We crossed Lake Laberge, made famous by Robert Service's poem "The Cremation of Sam McGee." Not much snow covered it, as most had blown off, but there was enough for the dogs that they could run easily with their booties on. If it was glare ice, I would have stopped to take their booties off so their nails could grip the ice to run. The sun was getting low in the sky, and we started passing teams that had pulled off the trail and bedded down. This confirmed my calculations were correct; we were around the halfway point to Braeburn. We continued passing various camped teams, most mushers calling out a greeting as we passed. I wanted to stop the team where we would be on our own so the dogs would get a better rest. I waited until I saw a quiet spot that looked perfect, despite Andy's annoyance that we didn't stop when we saw the first camped team. Andy loves his straw, and once he sees a team camping on straw, he is all about getting into his own straw bed.

Our camping spot was stunningly beautiful, large pine trees created a backdrop and shelter. I stopped the team and sunk my hook to hold them in place, calling Lily and Strider over off the trail. The snow was crazy deep, so I stomped around as quickly as I could, packing it down as much as was possible before unstrapping the bale of straw from my sled and shaking it out for the team. They eagerly went about digging and pawing my efforts to make their beds just perfect and then happily flopped down in the fresh straw. The snow was so fluffy, it wouldn't hold my snow hook, so I ended up sinking it just off the side of the trail where I could get a grip in the hard pack.

Dogs settled, I grabbed a bag of frozen salmon and handed each dog a piece to munch on as I started cooking them a hot meal. Grabbing my cooker, I filled the pot with snow, lit the fire, and put the lid on it so it would melt. While I was waiting, I went back up the dogs and started removing their booties and checking their feet. Everyone looked great, and, since they weren't really very tired yet, I got lots of licks.

Water boiling, I dumped in the frozen ground beef and, 10 minutes later, we had a nice hot stew. I laid out their bowls and scooped kibble in the bottom of each bowl and then ladled steaming beef stew over the kibble. It was almost dark now, and the warm day was quickly turning into a very cool night. The food cooled as I walked up to the dogs to serve them dinner, so it was warm by the time they were lapping it up. Everyone ate quickly, which is always a great sign. Bowls collected, I placed them back in the cooker and sat down on it. I wanted to stay here another three hours at least. Normally, I would stretch out in the straw with the dogs, but I was still too wired from the start, and it wasn't even 6 p.m. yet; no way I would be able to sleep or even lie still.

The dogs obviously felt the same way. They would take turns getting up, stretching, and redigging their beds, looking around and then flopping back down. As they would hear a team approaching, they would be up on their feet watching and ready to follow that team down the trail. We don't see teams other than our own on our home trails, so they were excited to see all these other dogs out here running, too. I found myself pulling out my watch every 10-15 minutes hoping more time had passed.

After the third team went by and everyone was up barking and howling to go, I gave up the notion of trying to get them to rest any longer. A good thing, too! As they heard the fourth team approaching, Lily and Strider took matters upon themselves and swung the team back to the trail. I didn't try to fight them; I was just as anxious to get moving again. I threw the cooker and a few other items I had out into the sledbag, pulled the hook, and we were off again.

Dusk was long gone and I had my headlamp on, but I didn't need it. The sky was so bright, I turned it off and even then I could see the trail just fine. The first hints of a show of Northern Lights started to appear in the sky, and I hoped my nephew and nieces who had spent three nights trying to see Northern Lights were going to be out to see them tonight before they headed back to Ontario. The show got stronger as we travelled; greens, blues, purples moving across the sky, shimmering, swirling, moving. I don't think I could ever grow tired of watching the Northern Lights. The dogs love watching them, too, and, as we ran, I would see them glance up to watch the show.

Blitz caught my attention. I turned my headlamp on to watch him more closely. He was favouring his front left leg ever so slightly. I stopped the team and sunk my hook to go up and check him. His bootie was fine, no snow between his pads, no evidence of anything. I moved his leg around carefully to check his wrist, shoulder, and elbow and got no reaction. Maybe he had just stepped wrong. I headed back to the sled and pulled the hook and we were off again. He seemed fine for about a mile and then I noticed it again. I went up and checked and still nothing. I decided to let him ride in the sled until we got to Braeburn and a vet could check him. Since we were stopped and it was close to snack time, I grabbed a bag of steak and tossed everyone a chunk. They munched happily as I moved gear around in the sledbag to make room for Blitz, putting down a blanket on top of the gear so he could be comfortable. Unsnapping him from the line and lifting him into the sled, he didn't resist at all and settled right in as I zipped the sled bag up around him so just his head was sticking out to watch the team.

A few miles later, Northern Lights still dancing, Maverick caught scent of the checkpoint and his tail went up. Everyone, following his lead, picked up their pace, all ears and eyes focused on what was just down the trail. A short while later, I started to hear sounds from the checkpoint. I turned my headlight back on so the volunteers would see us approaching and, as we came around a bend in the trail, I saw the checkpoint lights ahead of us.

The team was flying now. We always look incredible coming into a checkpoint! It was just before midnight, and I stepped on my brake to stop the team where the checker awaited us. She handed me her clipboard and I signed us into Braeburn. I saw Tanya and Ward nearby at one of the barrels that had a huge fire going in it for volunteers and handlers to stay warm as they waited for teams. The dogs were lunging into their harnesses and howling and carrying on, not a whole lot different than at the start. It sure looked impressive! The checker asked if we were staying, and I said yes. She looked at the team going crazy and back to me like I didn't have a clue what I was doing, but I nodded again, saying yes, we would be staying. One by one, she asked me to show her all my mandatory gear as she checked them off on her list.

I asked if a vet could please come have a look at Blitz when they had a minute, and she assured me she would send one right over. Volunteers went to the front of the team and ran in front of us to show us where our camping spot would be for the night. Straw and our drop bags were quickly tobogganed over to us by helpful volunteers, and I started shaking out the straw for the beds. As crazy as they had been a few minutes ago, with straw and the sight of all the other teams quietly sleeping, they were pawing through the straw and curling up, happily agreeing to the idea!

The pattern that would become total habit over the next 900 miles every time we stopped began: give the dogs a snack, start the cooker, pull off booties and look after feet while it heated. Feed dogs, get them settled, and check them again, then—and only then—go and get myself some food.

A team of veterinarians came over and asked if I would like them to look at the team. I nodded and pointed out Blitz and told them what I had seen. They checked every dog and spent extra time with Blitz, whose shoulder was a tiny bit stiff. They recommended massage and ointment and offered to check him again before I left. I thanked them and said yes, please. All the other dogs looked great, they said. As I worked, Tanya stood at the back of the sled. One of the rules for handlers is that they can stand at the back or front of the team but couldn't move from there and absolutely could not help the musher or interact with the dogs. Tanya said this was the hardest part of the whole race, having the dogs look at her with confusion, wondering why she didn't come over and give them some love. Only one handler was allowed at the team at a time, so Ward was waiting over by the fire with other handlers and volunteers. Dogs cared for and snuggled in, sleeping soundly, I headed to the lodge with Tanya and Ward.

It was likely around 1 a.m. at that point, but walking inside the small restaurant, we were slammed by both a wave of heat and a hive of excitement and activity. Race judges, communications folks, and veterinarians for the race were all in there with computers and phones. Photographers and PR folks were there writing, posting, and working, and then add in all the mushers and their families, handlers, and the place was absolutely packed. Winter gear hung and lay everywhere as a huge barrel wood stove pumped out heat. It was a challenge finding chairs and a spot at one of several long tables to sit down. Ward grabbed a chair from one table, some folks shoved down further at their table, and we squeezed in. Making our way to the counter to order food was like trying to move through a packed nightclub. Tanya headed up and made her way to order us food. While she and Ward had been waiting for me for several hours, the place was so busy, they hadn't gone in yet. The owner, as I found out later, was gruffly taking orders and asked Tanya if she was with a musher. She nodded and he said, "his meal is free." If you have never had the pleasure of stopping at Braeburn Lodge, let's just say you will never leave hungry. From the hamburger the size of a plate to the cinnamon buns that will do two people for a meal, Braeburn is a favoured checkpoint with all.

Food polished off, I went out and quickly checked the dogs again. They were all sound asleep, as more teams had joined the huge field of camping mushers since I'd gone inside. The teams that were running the shorter 300-mile version of the Yukon Quest, who had started their race after the 1,000-mile teams, were starting to arrive now, too. I grabbed my sleeping bag, hoping I could catch at least an hour or two of rest. Saying goodnight to Tanya and Ward as they headed to the truck, a volunteer showed me to the bunkhouse where mushers were sleeping. I asked her to wake me up in two hours.

I went in quietly so as not to wake the other mushers, closing the door and standing, waiting for my eyes to adjust to the dark. From my left, a heavy French accented voice commented, "not very comfortable in here!" This was my first introduction to Didier Moggia. I spotted an empty bunk and went over to it; the bedding was damp and cold. I stretched out my sleeping bag, took off my heavy outer suit and boots, and laid down. My French friend had seemingly fallen asleep, it seemed, and snores were echoing off the bunkhouse walls from mushers. He was right. It was freezing in here. It felt colder in here than outside, if that was possible; apparently there was no heat. I tossed and turned, trying to block out the sound—snoring drives me nuts at the best of times! After 30 minutes, I couldn't take anymore and got up.

Sleep was going to be impossible in here. I quickly put back on my boots and fleece coat and headed outside. Our truck would be quieter and way warmer than that bunkhouse!

I walked across the parking lot to where I saw our truck where Tanya and Ward were trying to catch some sleep. I knocked on the window and they quickly woke up. Ward rolled the window down and I felt the heat instantly rush out to meet me from the cozy warmth of the truck cab. "I'm going to sleep in the back seat of the truck for an hour," I said. "The bunkhouse is cold as hell, and the snoring is loud enough to wake the dead."

"You can't! You will be disqualified!" Tanya replied, and Ward nodded in agreement. I glared at both of them. Easy for them to say, sleeping in a warm, comfortable truck! They were right, of course, but I was furious with both of them for not being more understanding. Without another word, I turned and headed back to the bunkhouse, hearing the snoring before I even opened the door to go back in. For the next hour I tossed and turned. I managed to doze off a couple of times but would be quickly awakened by the snoring or the door opening as another musher left or entered or a checker came in to wake a musher up at the time they had requested. I gave up on any chance to get sleep here and got up before I had asked for a wake-up call. Tanya came over and got a grunt in response to her inquiry of whether I'd gotten any sleep. We headed over to check the dogs. They, at least, despite all the teams coming and going, were curled up in their straw looking nice and warm with their coats on and sound asleep. None of them even stirred at our approach. Sleep was more important for them than me anyway, especially this early in the race.

We headed back to the Lodge for coffee, and Tanya ordered me breakfast. I have never seen any place serve up as much food as Steve does at his lodge. Belly full of a delicious breakfast (not that I could eat a fraction of it all) and the first light of dawn showing across the horizon, my spirits improved. I headed out to get the dogs their breakfast so we could start getting ready to head back out on the trail. Overnight, the 300-mile teams had continued pulling into Braeburn, and between the 1,000-mile teams still there and the 300-mile teams, I have never seen so many dog teams camped out together before in my life. It was an amazing sight.

Cooker fired up and warming the water Braeburn Lodge kindly allowed mushers to use, the dogs' warm soup would be ready in no time without having to melt snow first. I started repacking my sled while the water heated. While my core gear from sleeping bag, axe, cooker, snowshoes, etc., remained with me the whole race, at every checkpoint I restocked my sled from my drop bags with dog kibble and meat, booties, food, and handwarmers for myself. I don't always need them, but every drop bag also has extra plastic for the sled runners as well as fresh socks and underclothes for me in case I get wet. I always send and pack tons of food for the dogs. I would far rather carry an extra couple of pounds of food than worry about running out. I have never understood mushers who spend so much money and time to enter these races and then shortchange on the amount of food they carry. During the Iditarod last year, several times I shared the extra dog food I had with me with teams that were running a bit short on food.

*Lily, Aster and Hosta howl at the front of the team
as we prepare to leave*

The next run to Carmacks was 75 miles, so we would break it
into two runs, stopping for a four-hour rest at the halfway point.

I would tie a bale of straw to the top of my sled again before leaving here so that I could make the dogs a nice comfortable bed out on the trail to nap for a few hours in the afternoon sun. Tanya stood at the back of the sled as per the rules and we chatted about the last run and the next one as I repacked the sled. The water was now steaming, so I dumped in the ground beef to let it thaw and start breaking up. The sled was now all packed and ready to go. I checked the runners, but they were still fine. No need to change plastic yet. I grabbed my container of fuel for my cooker and walked over to the lodge to fill it up. The Quest provided a free tank at every checkpoint for mushers' use. By the time I got back, the soup was almost ready. A veterinarian came by and asked if I needed them to check any dogs on the team. I said they were welcome to, that Blitz was the only one I specifically wanted checked. We both went up to Blitz, and he gently rotated his leg. While it didn't appear that it bothered Blitz at all, it was still stiff. The vet said it would probably work out while we got moving again. I wasn't as convinced and certainly didn't want Blitz to have to ride in the sled all the way to Carmack's if it didn't work out. I made the decision that he would be dropped from the team and stay here with Tanya and Ward. I signed the official paperwork that Blitz was off the team, and I was down to a team of 13 dogs.

Blitz didn't look all that happy with me when I unsnapped him from the line and Ward came with a leash to take him to the truck. I was second guessing myself. Not that I could—I had already signed the papers—but as I watched him walk, he was still quite stiff on that leg. I watched Ward bend over and pick him up, carrying him the rest of the way. He would be in good hands with Tanya and Ward. Another thing I love about the Quest, as soon as you decide to drop a dog from your team, they are back with your handlers and your truck instantly.

Soup ready, I lined the dogs' bowls up beside each other and poured some kibble in each bowl, then I took the ladle and stirred the soup so it was mixed evenly and poured a full ladle into each bowl. The dogs were awake now, smelling and hearing breakfast. They lazily took turns getting up to stretch before curling back up in their warm straw, most with their eyes on me. I grabbed several bowls at a time and, working from leaders back, put a bowl in front of each dog. Every one of them dove into their food, and every bowl was licked clean in no time. Collecting the bowls, I packed them back in the cooker and packed it back into my sled, leaving two bags of new booties on the top of the sled bag as I zipped it closed. While the sun wasn't up yet, it was now bright and I could work easily without a headlamp. I decided I would grab one more coffee to go before we headed out, thanking the volunteers we passed as Tanya and I went back to the lodge, quickly grabbed a coffee, and then went back to the team. I grabbed the bags of booties and headed up to Lily and Strider. Gloves off, I started the painstaking task of putting a bootie on every paw. The dogs are so used to it, most just lift their paw for you, and some won't even get up; they just hold out their leg. As I reached the back dogs, Lily and her sons Aster and Hosta sat and watched me work, starting a beautiful howl in unison. It was time to get back on the trail. They had watched enough teams pull out since they had awakened. The day was in full swing now!

Tanya went to find the checker so I could sign out. I got on the sled and pulled the snowhooks as Ward took the front of the team to lead them through all the other teams still camped and back to the trail. We reached the pilons and stop sign just before the road crossing, and Tanya and the checker were there waiting for us. With a quick look through the top of my sledbag to make sure all the required gear was there, she nodded and handed me the clipboard to officially sign out of Braeburn. The time I signed out would be recorded in the stats for fans and the race. Tanya ran ahead to take some pictures, and Ward ran at the front of the team to the road crossing. More volunteers were on the road, shoving snow so the runners of the sled wouldn't get too scraped up crossing the pavement, and also stopping traffic. The team were all fired up, tails flagging high and charging hard to get moving. I high-fived Tanya as we passed her on the other side of the road, and we were off into the forest again at 10:30 a.m.

7

The Mayor

The sun rose on a lovely day with temperatures slowly rising to make things very pleasant. Much of this run was river running, which was not the dogs' favourite, as they can see so far ahead of them it doesn't seem very exciting to not have the suspense of what is around the next corner compared to the trails we ran. The plus side today, though, was that we had teams passing us regularly as the 300-mile teams pulled out of Braeburn. Since they were doing 300 miles, they were moving a lot faster than us. Every time one of those teams passed us, the dogs would get all excited to start chasing them. But we had our own schedule to run, and I was the spoil sport that wouldn't let them go faster than they should. I would often get looks of disgust thrown over their shoulders at being the party pooper from the chase game.

I stopped to snack the dogs two hours after we left Braeburn, a quick frozen piece of steak to each, then we were off again. Every two hours after that, we would also stop for a quick break and snack. The first couple hundred miles I find the toughest, as the dogs and I get into the groove and routine of the trail. On the plus side, I wasn't super tired yet, and, for the dogs, the trail and race were new, so we were all still running on excitement.

We would see the occasional cabin on the riverbank as we passed by, some with signs stuck in the snow/ice wishing the YQ teams good luck. Later in the afternoon, we reached approximately the halfway point between Braeburn and Carmacks, and I found a good place to pull the team off the trail and bed down for a nice nap. I unstrapped the bale of straw from the top of the sled and started shaking it apart. The dogs were quick to help me dig apart the straw and make it into a nice bed that they approved of. I was already getting used to the routine that we would continue for the next 900 miles when stopping, and I would only get more efficient at completing the tasks quickly. Dogs fed and napping, I curled up in the straw with Lily and Strider. We were off the trail a ways, but we could still see teams going by; the dogs didn't bother to look up from their nap, which was a great sign they, too, were getting into the routine. Straw time meant rest and sleep time.

I dozed off and on in the sun, despite the -20°C temperature. I awoke to find dusk upon us and the temperature dropping quickly. We also had company now. Didier had stopped close by with his team. It was crazy how quickly the temperature was dropping, and I figured we were in for another -40°C night at this rate. Didier mentioned how cold it was and suggested starting a fire. I normally don't take the time to make a fire when I'm camping but agreed this time, and we gathered some wood. He decided he would use his remaining fuel to start the fire quickly. Before I had a chance to question that, he was pouring it on and dropping a match onto it. We had a fire alright! For about 30 seconds, and then had nothing as the fuel burned off and didn't spark into the damp wood. We finished the last of our rest without the warmth of a fire.

I offered the dogs another quick meal and then we were back on the trail headed for Carmacks. If all went well, we would be pulling in there around midnight. The dogs were excited to get going again, and having Didier's team with us made for extra excitement; and, of course, following the teams they had seen or heard pass over the last several hours. The nice thing with running at night on river runs was that the dogs were able to stay more focused as they didn't see so far ahead. My headlamp beam became their guide, and that helped them focus on short sections of trail. I also found it easier to concentrate when we ran at night. About an hour into the run, Jed started favouring one leg slightly. I stopped and went up to check if he had picked up a snowball in his pad or anything else that could be causing him discomfort. I found nothing. Jed hadn't been his normal happy-to-go, laid-back self that day. I think he was already missing his brother and best friend Blitz. I decided to let him ride into Carmacks in the sled to make sure the leg was fine. Jed didn't mind riding at all. Leave it to Maverick to pick up the scent of a checkpoint. With his tail set higher and increasing pace, which the team, as usual, picked up on, I knew we were only, at most, 10 miles from Carmacks. An hour later, as we came around another bend in the river, I saw the lights of the village ahead of us. We arrived right before midnight, as I had hoped, with Didier and his team arriving just a few minutes ahead of us.

Tanya and Ward were waiting for us. They had cleaned up after the team before leaving Braeburn, raking up all the straw—which, in Braeburn, is welcomed as bedding for the resident pigs and horses—and packing up what I had not needed from my drop bags. They also cared for Blitz, Loretto, and Governor before driving over to Carmacks to meet up with me again. The lives of handlers is much more boring than the lives of mushers! For me, it was so wonderful compared to the Iditarod, knowing that I would see them in every checkpoint except Eagle, which was not accessible in the winter by road.

After signing in and having the checker make sure all my mandatory gear was accounted for, Ward led the way to where the team would camp right beside the community centre and outdoor roofed arena. The community was kindly allowing the Quest to have full use of their community centre.

Carmacks is a First Nation village where the Yukon River and Nordenskiold River come together. It started out as a single cabin settlement back in the 1800s with George Carmacks building the first cabin that was his home. He tried his hand at mining and trading with the local Native residents, who had lived on this land for an incredible 10,000 years. It is said that in that cabin, George had collections of books, from literature to science, and even an organ. He ended up abandoning that settlement after several years from lack of gold and moved further north where he would become part of the three men who discovered the gold at Bonanza Creek in 1897, which set off the Klondike Gold Rush. This homestead to the south, though, would end up becoming a village and named after him. The village today has a population of around 500 residents.

The volunteers showed me where to park the team and where I would find straw and my drop bags, all set out alphabetically so mushers could quickly find theirs. Retrieving straw first to get the dogs resting, I unzipped Jed from the sledbag and walked him up to go back on the line with the other dogs. His limp was hardly noticeable now. The night had gotten cold quickly, with the temperature falling to around -40°C. The dogs took no time snuggling down in their straw as I worked on taking booties off and massaging feet as I waited for the water to heat. Three veterinarians came over and asked if now was a good time to look over the team. I said certainly. They asked if I had any concerns with any particular dog, and I mentioned Jed's leg. They carefully examined it but found nothing wrong with it and said it was likely soft tissue and to give it a good massage, that he should be fine to continue on with the team by morning. I wasn't as sure but agreed to try and see how he was doing come morning.

The team snooze in their straw during a break

The dogs all wolfed down their food—other than Jay not eating his frozen salmon, which was normal. Chores done and dogs all fast asleep with their blankets over them, I followed Tanya back into the community centre for some food and maybe some sleep that night. The cafeteria was always open and staffed with volunteers while mushers were coming through 24 hours a day and served up all the home-cooked food mushers could eat with no shortage of deserts and snacks to take with them as well. Handlers and race fans could purchase any of the food. The gym was open for handlers to lie down and sleep in, and one of the sports equipment rooms was cleared out for mushers to sleep in a fairly quiet place. Exercise mats were available for everyone to sleep on.

I peeled off my layers of outer gear, putting them and my boot liners on a rack with tons of other mushers' gear to hopefully dry a bit over the next couple of hours. After a great hot meal and visit with Tanya and Ward, I picked up my sleeping bag and, tucking it under my arm, headed into the gear room for some sleep, asking the volunteer to wake me in two hours. The race had already started to spread out. I heard officials call it a big python that just ate; a few front runners at the head, most of the teams the bulge in the middle, and some at the back. The checkpoint was way quieter than Braeburn had been, and, as I laid down on a mat, I was quickly asleep with a few other mushers in the room. Tanya stayed up to keep an eye on the dogs and make sure I didn't oversleep while Ward went to get a bit of sleep himself in the truck.

It seemed like I had just fallen asleep when someone was shaking me, gently whispering it was time to get up. I sure didn't want to… I laid there for a few minutes before slowly getting up and feeling the effects of sleeping on the floor as my whole body felt stiff. I rolled up my sleeping bag and quietly left the room so as to not wake the other sleeping mushers. Tanya was waiting for me in the hall and said she had checked the dogs several times and they were all sleeping soundly. It was still dark as I drank a coffee and started putting gear back on to go outside. I doubted it had warmed up at all the last few hours, but at least the gear I was putting on was warm and dry again!

The dogs were all still sound asleep, and I worked quietly to start repacking the sled and to get their meal ready for them. They smelled the food, though, and started to stir as I placed a bowl of warm soup in front of them. They each eagerly finished their food. I packed up the cooker and bowls, putting the rest of the hot soup in my cooler to have for their next meal down the trail, and got their booties out to start getting ready to go. Dawn was starting to brighten the horizon a little as I worked. The dogs were in a routine now and just held their paws for me to check and bootie. It took me what seemed like forever in those temperatures to bootie the dogs. I did several with bare hands and then stuck my hands back in my big mitts with hand warmers in them to warm up before I did the next couple. Finally, booties all on, I went to grab a quick coffee while Tanya went to find the checker, and I signed out of Carmacks, also signing the dropped dog sheet for Jed. He still seemed a bit sore and he was missing his brother, so he would stay with Tanya, Ward, and Blitz. I was sure he and Blitz would be happier together anyway.

As I zipped up my sled bag Ward commented that my big mitts were sitting on the hockey rink board beside me. Baffled

I glanced at my sled and shook my head, they weren't mine, mine were on my sled bag, right where they should be. But a pair identical to mine were sitting there. A musher had left them behind. Ward took them into the officials quickly so they could be sent up the trail to McCabe Creek. Someone was sure going to be missing them with this cold.

With a hug to Tanya and a "see you in Pelly" to Ward, the team was up, shaking off the straw in their coats, and stretching. We were moving again, but it would take them a few miles to fully wake up and hit their stride.

We dropped down on the river in the early morning light, and, as Tanya told me later, she stood on the riverbank watching us go until we disappeared around the river bend. A veterinarian stood quietly beside her watching us go and, as we disappeared out of sight, commented, "I just love watching traditional northern dogs travel this trail. It's like watching history come to life right in front of you."

The run was easy terrain, mostly river and wetland running. It was flat with not much sign of wildlife, and, with the teams starting to spread out, not many teams, either. Being day three, the dogs and I were hitting a routine now: travel, eat, sleep, and repeat. Everything seemed natural at this point. My plan again was to break this run into two sections; camping about 40 miles into the run would work perfectly and leave us napping in the afternoon sun and starting travel again with the change of light as dusk fell, which the dogs always loved.

We covered 40 miles steadily, dogs and I content. It was just one of those peaceful, uneventful runs. Sometimes those runs are nice, too. The trail led off the river and up the bank, and I could see a homestead not far off with tons of old equipment scattered around, possibly a farm? Checkers and a veterinarian were outside, so this must have been McCabe Creek. Not an official checkpoint, but a dog drop for anyone needing to drop a dog from their team and, of course, the support of a race official and a veterinarian if needed. I decided this was a perfect spot to stop, since it was about halfway to Pelly.

The dogs were quick to bed down in the straw I had packed as I shook it out for them and then went about taking off their booties and fixing them a hot meal. I snacked as I cooked for them and had company to visit with in the race personnel. Dogs fed, another man approached to chat. His eyes struck me first. While he was an older man with a white beard and the look of a miner, his blue eyes jumped with energy, fun, and a love of life. He welcomed me to McCabe Creek and introduced himself as the mayor. I was pleased to meet him, and we chatted about the dogs, the trail, and the Yukon for some time. At one point, he told me he had a daughter that was looking for a good husband that I should meet and that he was making me the honorary deputy mayor of McCabe. I mentioned I was already married and he winked at me, saying, "Well, two wives are better than one!" I choked. Wait until Tanya hears about this conversation. Perhaps stopping in McCabe had not been such a great idea... Not wanting to offend him, I mentioned I should try to get a bit of sleep before we headed out, and he ushered me to the house that looked like it was being renovated where long tables had been set up for mushers with food, coffee, and various drinks. There were also cots laid out for us to sleep on. I thanked him again for his kindness and laid down for an hour's rest.

The sun was setting as I woke and went to get the dogs ready to go. Time to get back on the trail to find Pelly Crossing, ideally before midnight again. My new friend was there and wished us a good run and told us he would meet up with us somewhere down the trail again. I really wasn't sure what to make of our conversation but was sure Tanya and Ward would get quite a chuckle out of his offer for another wife and being made a deputy mayor.

We were back on the river again travelling well. Didier had come into McCabe shortly after me and was pulling out about the same time. I enjoyed the French man's company. While we wouldn't run together, it was nice knowing a team was nearby.

When the dogs ran on rivers and flat terrain, I took my ski pole out of my sled and alternated poling with one hand and then pushing with one foot to help the dogs along. It was a smooth motion: pole, kick, pole, kick. It also served to help me stay warmer with the activity. I also watched the dogs carefully; we had spent so many miles together, I could pick up a change in how they were feeling almost instantly. I found myself watching Andy. My gorgeous large as life big red boy was carrying his tail a bit lower than normal, and his ears didn't have their normal alertness to them. I stopped the team and, sinking the hook, went up to check him. His eyes were the next thing that told me he just wasn't feeling himself. I checked his dehydration, his gum colour, his capillary refill, and they all seemed fine. But something was off. I didn't know what, but he was going to ride with me until we got to Pelly and a veterinarian could give him a full examination to be safe. The one issue with having tons of dogs on the same trail from all over North America is that one team can bring in a bug that the other dogs haven't been exposed to. Denis Tremblay, a French musher who had started the race, had scratched in Carmacks when his whole team came down with something.

Andy didn't seem to mind riding, and he curled up in the blanket I laid out in the sled bag for him as I zipped him safely inside. That in itself concerned me. Andy normally would be like the Tasmanian devil to try and keep in the sledbag. I took the time to snack the dogs since we had been running almost two hours since leaving McCabe Creek.

Any hint of the sunset was long gone and we ran under the clear sky, bright with the stars out in all their glory. An hour or so passed and I saw Maverick's nose shoot up, sniffing the air. Yup, right on time. We should be about 10 miles from Pelly Crossing. Shortly after, I could see the lights of cabins come into view along the river bank. People equals a checkpoint, and the team picked up their pace. We jumped off the river and it seemed we were running down a road. I saw barriers in front of us where the road was closed except for Yukon Quest teams. Beside the barrier, as we approached the community centre all lit up, I saw Tanya waiting outside to greet us and guide us into the area set aside for teams to rest. We were then greeted and signed in by an RCMP officer in uniform. The officers were helping out with teams at this checkpoint along with other volunteers. Veterinarians were also waiting to look over the team, and I mentioned my concern around Andy. They asked if I was considering taking him further and I said no. We took him out of the sled bag, and they took him inside to the area they had set up to examine him further but didn't seem overly concerned.

Team cared for and fast asleep, I followed Tanya into the community centre for food. A veterinarian came over and said Andy had a slight fever and cough but nothing that some medicine wouldn't fix. She would keep him with her overnight but said he would be fine to go with Ward and Tanya to Dawson in the morning. She assured me she would make sure a veterinarian checked him again as soon as they arrived in Dawson but that she really wasn't concerned at all and that he would be just fine. That was a huge relief.

Caring for the team in Pelly Crossing

Pelly Crossing was the home of the Selkirk First Nation. I was told that Pelly was built in the 1950s when a spot was needed for a bridge crossing when the Dawson Highway was built. Many of the residents of Fort Selkirk relocated here, and the community was home to about 300 residents. The local school did all the cooking at this checkpoint as a fundraiser. While mushers ate for free, handlers and everyone else paid a reasonable price for a great hot home-cooked meal. I was tired by the time I sat down and started dozing off while I was eating. Tanya kept nudging me, telling me to hurry and finish and then go get some rest. She asked if I was switching up leaders at all and I shook my head. Are you going to she asked? It was a fair question; we had worked hard all fall training various leaders. Maverick, Scully, and Charlie were all proving themselves to be fine young leaders, and switching them up would give Lily and Strider a mental break for sure, but Lily hated running anywhere else other than lead, and she and Strider ran and worked so well together, I didn't want to split them up. I answered that there was no need to yet.

I dozed off again sitting at the table and finally, shaking my head to wake up, I headed outside to check the team once more before trying to get some sleep myself. It was a cold night again, likely -40°C, and I shoved all the straw tightly in and around each of them as they slept to make sure they were warm. The Yukon Quest kindly provided a free bale of straw at every checkpoint for each team, but you could order and pay for more if you wanted it. We always had at least two bales and often three ordered for each checkpoint. I had often heard people say as they passed the team that we had the heaviest coated dogs in the race and that they were the team bedded on the most straw. My dogs were not going to be cold if it was in my power to make sure they were warm and sleeping comfortably!

Going back inside, I picked up my sleeping bag and headed to the small upstairs room they had set aside for mushers. It was dark and blissfully quiet with only a couple of mushers sleeping. I stretched out my sleeping bag and was out instantly. Despite my massive anxiety about the next section of trail, I slept soundly for the next two hours until the checker woke me up. I had asked her too. One more run, and then I could get a great sleep at the halfway point in Dawson. I lay in my sleeping bag for a bit, thinking about the next run; 200 miles to Dawson. I had never run more than 100 miles without stopping to resupply before, so 200 miles was beyond daunting.

I got up and went downstairs to find Tanya sitting at the table in the gym on her computer waiting for me. I grabbed another coffee and sat down with her. She turned the computer towards me, and I saw all the messages that had poured in the last few hours on our Facebook page to the team and me. I got inspired reading all the kind wishes and thoughts, and it gave me an extra push to get moving. I grabbed my gear off the drying racks and we headed outside to get the dogs another meal. I started emptying all the drop bags we had shipped to Pelly to sort out how much I could possibly fit into my sled. I started packing carefully, using every single inch of space. I didn't need any extra gear than what I was already carrying other than one more set of plastic for my runners which fit behind my sledbag anyway. It was all the dogs' food and booties. I packed as much as I possibly could, weighting between what they would want to eat most, as I couldn't pack everything we had sent. I pulled out my snowshoes, sliding them outside my sledbag between the stanchions of the sled to make more room. I pulled out my sleeping bag, bungee tying it to the top of my sled. That allowed several more bags of food to be packed. I attempted to zip up the sledbag; thank goodness the zipper was super heavy duty, as it took me working it up with great force to close. To say the sledbag was bulging was an understatement, and I was still worried I didn't have enough packed. Dogs fed, I headed back inside for one last coffee. Tanya tried to get me to eat some breakfast, but with anxiety tying my stomach in knots, there was no way I was eating that morning.

Didier had gotten up about 30 minutes after I did and he was packed and pulling his snowhook and gone. This was his second Quest, and he didn't seem concerned at all about this 200-mile run. I knew I was dragging my feet leaving. I should have been out of here 30 minutes before at least, but it was taking some work to get my courage up to leave. Shit, one of the qualifiers to get to come to the Quest/Iditarod was a 300-mile race, and that had 5 or 6 checkpoints. We were about to go 200 miles with no checkpoints.

RCMP officers in Pelly Crossing helping at the checkpoint

Finally, I convinced myself it was now or never. We had to get moving; waiting any longer, I was just torturing myself with "what if"s. I grabbed my hat, mitts, and thermos and headed for the door. Reaching the team, I started putting their booties on as quickly as I could. I wasn't going back inside again. Tanya went to find the checker, and I signed out at 7:09 a.m. Tanya told me Andy was on the truck with her and Ward and seemed much better already. They would find a vet to recheck him the second they rolled into Dawson. She looked me in the eye and said they would have the camp all set up for me and the dogs when I rolled in. They would see us in two days with clean clothes, a hot bath, and a burger and beer along with a warm bed for a good long sleep! I smiled, trying to reassure both of us all was good. I don't think I fooled her a bit. She hugged me, and I reached down to pull the snowhook. As I did, I glanced at all the extra food in the drop bags that wouldn't fit in the sled. I whistled at the team and they were up and shaking, happy to be on the move again. There were lots of people around that morning as we headed down the road, past a lovely old church, and dropped down onto the Yukon River, headed to Dawson.

8

The Three Stooges

A kilometre or so down the trail, a large bridge spanned the river and I stopped the team just before we reached it. I looked up at the road approaching the bridge, watching for our truck. I didn't want to talk to Tanya or Ward, just catch one more glimpse, smile, and wave as the truck went over the bridge. I didn't see them. I waited around 10 minutes until the dogs got annoyed at me and were done with waiting when we had just started to get moving again. Emotion welling up, I pulled the snowhook and let the dogs take us down the trail. The stupidest things can run through your mind when you are anxious and sleep deprived. I remember thinking "shit, they just decided to keep going." It never crossed my mind that they were still in the checkpoint, raking up and bagging all the used straw where the team had slept, packing up everything I had left behind from my drop bags on the truck, and then taking the dogs they were caring for, for a good walk/run before they started the 150-mile drive to Dawson City. Instead, I was just feeling sorry for myself and feeling forgotten. Sleep deprivation and the wilderness can wreak havoc on your emotions. It's why I say I've experienced some of my highest highs and lowest lows on these trails, and sometimes they are an hour apart.

The dogs, however, weren't letting my down mood bother them today. They were happy and feeling great on this sunny, calm day as it started to warm up, and it wasn't long before their good mood rubbed off on me. We were on the Yukon Quest trail headed to Dawson City on a stunning winter's day!

It was crazy running the river. You would think it would be totally flat, but at times I forgot I was even on a river as it seemed like you are climbing a hill. The trail became confusing at times, as old trail markers were still up and new trail markers missing, but Lily and Strider kept us on the right trail. By mid afternoon, trail markers led us off the river and up the insanely steep river bank. The climb up, while short, had some of the dogs on top of the bank while the sled was just leaving the river. We were in Stepping Stone right about noon, and I decided to stop and spend a bit of time there. I had been told by Didier and other mushers that the hospitably of Stepping Stone was amazing. There was a whole camp set up there with what looked like had been farm land at one time. As I pulled up, I saw Jerry and Didier's teams camped out napping in the warm sun. A family called Stepping Stone home, and they treated us like kings—whatever we wanted was there for us to eat. Fellow mushers Kyla and Christine arrived to join us a little while after I had the team cared for.

I only stayed about five hours, just long enough to feed the dogs and let them catch some sleep. I caught an hour or so myself as they had beds inside for us to crash on. As the sun was setting, it was time to get back on the trail and let the dogs enjoy running as day changed to night, at sunset, as they loved to do. Jerry pulled out about 30 minutes before Didier and I left together. Christine and Kyla were going to stay for a bit longer.

Didier and I travelled together for a while, but Didier pulled ahead as he was faster and that was fine. While it was nice knowing there were other teams in your general vicinity, I preferred travelling on my own without me or the dogs trying to run another team's schedule or pace. I unzipped my sledbag slightly. Tanya had bought me some additional snacks that she put in the sledbag at the start, and one of those was an 18" meat stick. I had been eyeing it up since the start but had been holding off eating it, savouring the thought of eating it for many miles now. Tonight seemed like the perfect night to enjoy it, and I pulled it out, zipping up the sledbag as I did so to keep as much frost out of it as possible. As we ran, I opened the end of the package and, with one hand holding the package, pulled the meat stick loose with my other hand. The very second the meat stick was out of the package, we passed a tree that overhung the trail. As it snapped out of the way, it caught my meat stick, and I watched in horror as my treat that I had been saving for four days flew through the air and disappeared into deep snow over 10 feet off the trail. The moment I had been savouring, my mouth already watering, and it was gone; there was no getting it back now. That was one of the most disappointing moments thus far in the race.

The hoar frost was horrible on this run; it was coating absolutely everything. The SPOT tracker the Yukon Quest had attached to the front of my sled, which allowed the race organization and the fans to follow each team as they travelled, was driving me nuts. It had a blinking light on it and, as the frost started coating it, the light became like a laser that blinded me. I reached over to wipe the frost off it several times, but, within minutes, it would be covered again with the light shining through annoying me. Finally, I'd had enough of it and stopped the team, set my hook, and kneeled down in the snow to deal with the light. Shutting it off seemed like the most obvious solution, so I did. Getting back on the sled and pulling the hook, the team and I continued down the trail in the dark with me feeling much happier with the stupid light dealt with. It never occurred to me as I turned that button off that there were real live people (including my wife) sitting and staring at computer screens watching me, thanks to that SPOT tracker, and who were going to frantically worry about the team and me throughout the night.

Several hours later, I caught up with Gerry and Didier who'd stopped to care for their dogs. I stopped to give my guys a rest and snack, too, and we enjoyed each other's company for a bit. We saw a headlamp approaching as a team caught up to us, and Kyla joined our party. Jerry asked her if she wanted to join us and she replied, "Yeah, I'll run with the 3 stooges!" Jerry, Didier, and I were all in our late 40s to 50s, and Kyla was in her 20s. Guess we looked like stooges to her.

I continued on and made camp a ways further down the trail so the dogs would get a better rest. We would rest for four hours and then continue on to the remote cabin which served as a Dog Drop called Scroggie. It was another cold night, I imagine around -40°C again, but I had brought straw, so the dogs were comfortable. I slept in my sledbag and likely caught an hour or so of rest. With the hoar frost still bad when I got up, the sledbag was coated in it, as was all my gear.

The dogs fed and rebootied and sled repacked, we were back moving again. Jerry and Didier passed us on this section and reached Scroggie before us. As we got close, dawn was setting in, and, as the sun rose, the warm glow of the early morning made everything seem warmer even if the mercury hadn't started to move yet. The dogs were trotting along happily, but, with the scent of something ahead, everyone picked up their pace and their tails. Shortly after, Scroggie cabin came into sight, and I saw Jerry's and Didier's teams bedded down.

Scroggie isn't much; calling it a cabin is too generous. It is a shack in the middle of nowhere. It has four walls made of plywood and a wood stove that billowed out heat. It was built by the race for a spot to host a veterinarian and race judge in case a team needed help. A float or ski plane could land on the river, and that is how the officials and gear got there and how dogs that were dropped would get back to Dawson to meet up with their handlers. Scroggie also represented the halfway point in the 200-mile stretch of trail. A hundred miles behind us, a hundred yet to go to reach Dawson. As I started bedding the team down, I was greeted by the officials and a vet went over the team, who were all doing great. I also was told about the annual iced beard competition, and I found myself staring into a camera getting my picture taken. Apparently, since Kyla and Christine were the only teams left to come in, I concluded the entries for the year and apparently had the dubious honour of winning. Kyla showed up a few minutes later.

We stayed 6 hours, the dogs getting another nice rest in the sun, but by 3 p.m., we needed to get moving. The problem was, you really didn't want to leave Scroggie because you were headed out for 100 miles of nothing except wilderness and huge climbs; plus, while lacking for size and amenities, the company made you not want to leave the warm shack. Everyone did their best to keep the tone light and jokes aplenty. Before leaving Scroggie, the race judge took my SPOT tracker and put fresh batteries in it and reattached it to my sled. I didn't think anything of it, as it was daylight still and it wasn't annoying me, but having my "husky" show up again on the Yukon Quest map was a huge relief to Tanya, our family, and friends, so they could see where I was and watch the team moving again.

We pulled out of Scroggie and dropped down onto the river, crossed it, then climbed up the other side. One thing about the Quest was that the drops off and on the rivers were crazy. You can drop 20-35 feet almost straight down. I remember saying to Tanya when she asked how the Quest trail compared to Iditarod trail that there were sections of trail worse than Iditarod's famed "Steps," and no one even mentioned them!

We were heading into the black hills and, wow, are they brutal. As we started up the big climb, I started to feel like I would never find the damned top. The switchbacks just kept going and going, and, since we were running it at night, there was no way to see how far up the top was. I'm not sure if that was a good thing or not... It seemed like we did over a dozen switchbacks. At one point, I glanced down and noticed a headlamp of another team working their way up behind us. I was a little jealous. It was always so much easier running up a big hill or mountain when you had a team in front of you, as your dogs want to catch the other team. We continued to climb to the top, and it seemed to take hours. I stopped several times to give the dogs a break and snacks. Since I was getting fed up with when we would ever reach the top, the dogs were as well. Finally, we reached the crest, and then we were heading along the top of the black hills, which was all forest. The team that had been gaining on us caught us as we reached the top, and I heard Kyla's friendly voice shouting out a greeting. As she did, my headlamp scanned the ground and I saw fresh moose tracks everywhere I looked. It looked like there was a herd of 500 moose stomping around up there. Kyla followed my headlamp and said, "How do you feel about running together for a while?" I normally don't run with other teams; they normally travel faster than our Sibes, and I find the dogs either moving faster than they normally would to keep up or me adjusting our run/rest schedule to match other teams. However, on strange trails in the middle of the night with moose everywhere, having two teams together sounded like a good plan. I said I thought it was wise to travel this section together, just in case.

We took a quick break to snack our teams, but my team was ready to go. Maverick smelled moose, God help me. Kyla was running Brent Sass's yearling team, and between her being so petite and a team of fast dogs, I'm sure she was riding her drag mat as we carefully moved along the trail. As we ran through the night, we were lucky (not according to Maverick) that we didn't see any moose.

At the base of King Solomon Dome, we decided it made sense to camp and let the dogs have a good rest before we started climbing the mountain. We all ended up camped together that night for several hours, Didier, Kyla, Jerry and me. I pulled out my sleeping bag and laid it out in my sledbag. I laid down to rest knowing I would only be able to try and sleep for about 60-90 minutes before the cold would start seeping into my sleeping bag. After the Iditarod last year and what happened when my sleeping bag froze shut with me in it, I never zipped my sleeping bag up again.

What we didn't know as we camped there that night was that Christine was not far behind us camped on her own. All the officials and fans assumed she was with us, as her tracker showed she was so close to all of us. Had she known and travelled only several miles further, she could have joined us that night and also travelled up King Solomon Dome and into Dawson with us. As it was, she didn't get to Dawson, and the trail breakers went to help her after she didn't show up later the next day. Dawson was as far as her journey went on this race.

We packed up and pulled our hooks to start working up the Dome around 5 a.m. We would get to Dawson City today, and I couldn't wait. The hospitality of Dawson City was legendary. The dogs would have an amazing rest, and, I won't lie, a hot bath and warm bed would feel really good! I tried to add up how much sleep I'd had got since the start five days ago. I figured it was roughly around 9-10 hours sleep in total, and most of that had been restless sleep—I was exhausted.

The others went first, as I knew we would be slower. It was a straight climb over a thousand feet long up the Dome. It didn't seem as bad as the Black Hill climb but still made any climb we did in Ontario look like an ant hill. As we finally reached the peak, we did a big, sweeping loop along the top of the mountain, which was about a kilometre across, going around a huge communication station and a small park before starting the long, sweeping decline. I glanced down and saw two of my friends' teams working their way down. I didn't want our dogs to chase them, so I hooked down to snack and wait a few minutes so they would be further out of the dogs' sights. Dawn was just starting to spread across the sky. It was beyond stunning. The dogs and I together that morning sat and watched the sunrise. It was one of the most beautiful scenes I had ever seen, as the sun rose and started lighting up a sea of mountain peaks one after the other. I've been accused of stopping to smell the roses on the trail. Well, today we stopped to watch the sunrise, and I will never forget that moment as long as I live, sitting there with my team.

Sun up, I pulled the hook, and the dogs were happy to start their way down the long, sweeping hill. We would drop almost 3,000 feet as we made our way to Dawson City, about 30 miles away. As we worked our way down, the snow seemed so strange. I was beyond sleepy. I put my little bicycle seat down to lean on for a few minutes to ease my back. I shut my eyes just for a minute…and woke with a start and a shock. It felt like I was in *The Twilight Zone*, if you remember that show. The team was standing still, every single dog looking back at me, the sled was standing still and we were going down a 45-degree incline. How was that possible? I stood up and tried to shove the sled, but it was like being on sand. The dogs just watched me, like, "Yup, it is impossible to move in this stuff!" Figuring the snow conditions had changed, I flipped my sled on its side to try a different kind of plastic. Different kinds of plastic slide better on different types of snow, temperatures, etc. I tried white, locked it in, flipped the sled back up and shoved—nothing, just as bad. I flipped it back over again, took off the white plastic, put on the black graphite. Flipped it back up and tried again—no difference. What bloody kind of snow was this?

Finally realizing that it didn't matter what type of plastic I put on, I started shoving the sled down the mountain. The dogs got up and started pulling and, between the 12 of us, we got to the base of King Solomon Dome. It would turn out part of the buzz in Dawson that if anyone found a type of plastic that worked on the snow coming down King Solomon Dome, no one's sleds would glide over it...

We were now travelling through the gold fields, and one of the creeks was Bonanza Creek, the creek that had sparked the Klondike Gold Rush over 100 years ago. As we traveled along the fields, I would look down the edges and there would be an excavator sitting 100 feet down in a gorge. You wouldn't know how the hell it ever even got out there. At one point, I saw one of the old steamboat type dredgers, possibly dating back 100 years, just abandoned in the middle of nowhere. Then you see mile upon mile of tailings from all the mining. It was absolutely mind boggling what I saw, and to picture how much the landscape had been changed from mining as mountains were literally moved in the search for gold. At one point, we came across a massive excavator blocking the trail, so big that one bucket load would have filled a huge mining dump truck. The excavator had been left on the road to block the entrance to the mining operation for the winter to unwanted explorers. The trail went exactly where the excavator was—to be more specific the trail went under the boom of the excavator! The dogs looked at it like it was strange that the bucket of the excavator was on one side of us and the cab of the machine on the other as we ran under the boom. That was one of those times I wished I'd had a picture to show I wasn't hallucinating!

I could see Dawson in the distance, but it seemed to be taking forever to get there as we wound down trails and onto the Yukon River again, slowly coming into town. The team was in fine form, as they knew with this many buildings and people and smells, we had to be nearing a checkpoint. The trail headed back up the river bank right where a large old Sternwheeler sat perched on the river's edge. As we ran past it, we dropped down the other side of the bank and onto Front Street. Snow was spread on the side of the road, and a snowfence was put up to keep the teams away from cars. I could see the large gate welcoming Quest mushers to Dawson City, and people lined up to welcome us. I quickly picked out Tanya and Ward in the crowd. It was so great to see them; it had felt like forever, even though it had only been a little over two days. The 3 Stooges and Kyla had all arrived in Dawson City within an hour of each other, half of the race behind us, half before us—but first, a 36-hour rest for dogs and mushers, and that sounded like heaven!

The team dropping onto the street off the riverbank in Dawon City

9

Dawson City!

Tanya and I had visited Dawson City about 15 years ago on a trip we took from Whitehorse to Dawson and then over Top of the World Highway to Tok before heading south to Valdez, Haines and then back to Whitehorse. We drove into Dawson at dark in the pouring rain with the thermometer reading 3°C in August. We had quickly decided we could afford a cheap motel instead of camping as had been our plan. As we were driving through town looking for one, two guys stumbled out into the street off the boardwalk in front of us. Fists flying, I assumed they had gotten chunked out of the bar. Two guys duking it out in a muddy street in the pouring rain was our first image of this century-old famous gold town.

Things were much quieter for this visit, though. Many of the locals and miners headed to warmer parts of the world for the winter, and the town almost seemed deserted compared to the bustling hub of locals, miners, and tourists that it was in the summer.

Tanya was out to take pictures and greet the team and me as Ward knelt in the snow to give Lily and Strider some love as they came into the chute. It was wonderful for both the dogs and me to have a warm welcome after so many long miles. Hans handed me the clipboard, and we were officially signed into Dawson, the halfway point in the race. My sled was quickly checked for all mandatory gear, and jokes were made that it was looking a bit of a mess! A few more pictures and warm welcomes, and we were off to the campground across the Yukon River. I asked Tanya to come with me, and she hopped on one runner as Ward jumped into the truck to drive across.

Having grown up on Wolfe Island where, when we were young, people drove across the ice to the mainland all the time, driving on ice didn't seem that foreign, but it still seemed a bit strange to see the truck drive down a boat ramp and out onto the frozen Yukon River. As the dogs followed the truck across, I shared some of the stories from the past two days with Tanya—of the sunrise on King Solomon Dome, the mayor of McCabe Creek trying to marry me to one of his daughters, and then making me a Deputy Mayor. The challenge, the beauty, and yet the eeriness of running through the history and graveyard of the black hills and gold fields.

Crossing the Yukon River in Dawson City

The truck pulled up the boat ramp on the other side of the river, and Lily, Strider, and team trotted along behind them. As we climbed the hill and then turned right into the campground, Tanya filled me in on their adventures setting up the dogs' tent and the campsite. Ward parked the truck and jogged along beside us, since after the first team arrived in the campground, no vehicles were allowed in so that teams would have a quiet place to rest. The only exception was once a team left Dawson, their handlers were allowed to drive in to pack up their campsite so they could get back on the road headed to meet their team again in Alaska.

We arrived at our campsite, and I assured Ward and Tanya it looked great. We had no idea what we would need to make a campsite for the dogs when we left Ontario. We had been told there were trees you could tie off ropes to, to create a tent, but that some sites were more open and you couldn't depend on trees and you wouldn't know what site you were assigned until you arrived. We had packed 2x4s and 1x1 strapping in the truck, along with hammers, saw, and nails when we left Haliburton so that if no trees were close by, the tent could be built out of a wood frame with tarps secured over it.

Tanya and Ward building the dogs camp in Dawson City

Our home for 36 hours – dogs tent close to the river, Ward's in foreground

Ward and Tanya, with help from three lovely ladies who were volunteering at the Quest from Ontario, did a great job creating a shelter for the dogs with hammer, nails, wood, tarps, rope, and tie downs. It had to be open on both ends as per race rules, but large chunks of snow/ice had been stacked up a ways on the end of the shelter to provide a windbreak for the dogs. Four bales of lovely fresh straw had been shaken out inside the tent, with a chain running underneath to snap each of the dogs off to so everyone had their own space. As we unsnapped the dogs from the gangline and brought them inside the tent, Ward and Tanya got all the thanks they could hope for as the dogs delightedly started digging through all the straw, making their perfect nests, and settling down happily into them. Dogs all contently curled up in their straw beds, we pulled out the cooker and started a hot meal for them.

Ward asked me a bit later when we were outside the tent and I was thanking him for the great setup, "Have you ever built something with four women telling you how to do it?" I couldn't help it; I was doubled over laughing from the image. Ward gave me an annoyed stare and then joined in, although I have a feeling during the construction, he most certainly hadn't been in a laughing mood!

We also shook our heads as we saw firsthand how all the other mushers handlers had built their tents solely from tarps, wratchet straps, and ropes. Not a single person had a piece of lumber, hammer, or nails. Oh, how we stood out as rookies from Ontario!

In Dawson City, the rules go out the window for 36 hours. Handlers are not only allowed to help care for the dogs but are encouraged to do so. Tanya was encouraging me to head to the hotel room to start getting some sleep, but I wasn't the least bit tired at the moment and wanted to stay with the dogs for a while longer. As the dogs settled in, I lay in the straw with them, massaging, hugging, and just enjoying giving them TLC. As I was doing that, I was also sharing stories with Tanya and Ward of our adventures to this point.

With the dogs starting to close their eyes to sleep, I decided I should do the same. Thirty-six hours sounded like a long time, but veteran mushers had warned us it would go fast and to make sure we had a strict schedule for the 36 hours. We did to some point, but, never having done this before, we were flying a bit by the seat of our pants, too. Ward had Al Hardman's Hot Tent all pitched with the stove going inside and it was toasty warm. He would camp with the dogs tonight, and Christine was staying to help him. They had a schedule for feeding the dogs. I planned on getting 6-8 hours of sleep and jumped into the shower while Tanya went to get us food. I'm not sure a hot shower has ever felt as good as that one did! Followed up with a hamburger, fries, and onion rings, life had never seemed better as I crawled into bed. I don't even remember hearing Tanya leave as she headed back across the river to help with the dogs and see if Ward needed anything else. I also hadn't noticed that she was busy on the phone behind my back. Turns out one of our staff had been in an accident with our pickup truck back home and while, thankfully, no one had been hurt and no dogs had been on the truck, we very quickly needed to replace that truck to keep tours rolling. Tanya never tells me anything that is going on at home that she thinks would take my focus away from the race or cause worry, but I hadn't figured that out yet at that point, so when she all of a sudden said I think I forgot to put the drop bars up on the truck, I said I would go do it. The second I was out the door, she was on the phone trying to arrange for a new truck.

*Dawson City! Rest time for dogs and me,
dogs snuggled down and all content*

I slept 11 hours straight before waking up hungry, not sure I had ever slept that long before. We got a huge breakfast, all the while seeing lots of familiar faces, both mushers and handlers, at the hotel's restaurant before heading over to the campground in the dark around 6 a.m. to help Ward look after the dogs. Tanya grumbled again about how much she hated driving on ice.

Ward said the dogs heard us coming about five minutes before we reached the tent, so they were all awake, tails wagging, happy to see us. Ward had done a great job looking after them and he said they had all eaten everything he put in front of them. We started taking them out for runs to stretch and make sure they didn't get too stiff and sore from resting. The dogs enjoyed the fun of just going for runs up and down the campground on leashes as they checked out the other dogs that were still in the campground. When we were at the campsite switching dogs around 7 a.m., out of nowhere about six black SUVs went down the campsite road, one right after another, disappearing into the dark. We all looked at each other, confirming we had all seen what we thought we did. Tanya put a leash on Maverick and I put a leash on Charlie and off we went for another run. As we got near the end of the road where the restart of the race was, we saw all the vehicles again. There had to be about 20 big guys in military uniforms all with communication ear pieces in. Maverick dragged Tanya over to an older gentleman in a blue coat who had a huge smile on his face. He leaned over and gave Maverick a pet and commented on what a beautiful animal he was (Maverick agreed). With that, we kept going on our run, having no idea what the heck was happening in the closed Dawson City campground. Turns out our newly appointed Governor General David Johnson was in Whitehorse and had requested to come out early before his departure to see a team head back out on the trail of the Quest. Johannes was scheduled to come off his 36-hour layover at 7:30 a.m., so Mr. Johnson with his security detail were there to watch him go. Maverick has a way of making friends wherever he goes!

The weather had turned since our arrival the day before. It had snowed hard all night and continued to do so in the morning. There was already likely six inches of fresh snow, and the wind was picking up. While the campground was sheltered, the river sure wouldn't be.

We switched dogs again, and, while we were running them this time, Wade Marrs came off the river, saying he had been running for 9 hours. Having not been able to find Forty Mile in these conditions, he had turned back. He said it was so bad out there, he was scratching. No way he was going back out again…

Shortly after, Cliff and his team came back in, saying they couldn't see anything. Tamara was the next one set to leave, but she said there was no way she was going out into that storm when two teams had already turned back. So the decision was made that everyone coming off their 36 hours today would all wait and leave together that night, when I was done my 36 hours. Six teams would leave and travel together up the Yukon River into the storm headed for Forty Mile.

The rest of the day passed quickly. With all the dogs exercised, we headed to get the sled ready. In the warmth of the garage, everything was repacked, and new plastic was put on the runners. This run, while having several hospitality stops, would be 150 miles before we could restock our sleds with drop bags in Eagle, and I had every spare inch of area filled with food and gear. It took all three of us to get the zipper closed on the bag and I, not for the first time in this race, was grateful for the heavy zipper in the bag and hoped it would hold everything together. I wasn't as nervous as when I left Pelly, though. That had been 200 miles, and we had come into Dawson with lots of extra food left. Packing the same way and 50 miles less, we would be fine for supplies.

Tanya insisted I try to get a few more hours of sleep before heading out, and, while I thought I was way too nervous to sleep, I did manage to get a couple of hours while she ran around getting last minute items together.

I was not only nervous for what the team and I were about to head out into though, I was also nervous for Tanya and Ward. The job of being a Yukon Quest handler is intense and a team's success or failure is greatly impacted by the handlers they have. While I would be running 300 miles to reach Circle, Tanya and Ward would be packing up the whole camp and then heading out on an almost straight through drive of 1100 miles to meet up with me again. A drive that would go through incredibly remote and dangerous sections of Alaska and the Yukon.

Four p.m. found us back in the campground. We would be off our layover at 7 p.m., and everyone was starting to get ready. Dogs had another meal and more massages and quick runs. I double-checked the sled yet again that I hadn't forgotten anything. The snow had pretty much let up, but the wind, if anything, was getting worse and making the river a ground blizzard.

Teams started going by our campsite headed for the restart. It was time. I got all my gear on and then, with four of us harnessing dogs, it didn't take long to have everyone on the gangline ready to go. With Ward running beside Strider and Lily, we headed down the road to the river. Jerry was in the chute in front of us, and veterinarians and checkers were there making sure all was good and signing each of us out. I signed beside my name; we could go whenever we were ready, as our 36 hours was up. I watched Jerry go down the riverbank out into the middle of the river before turning with the trail to head parallel to the river bound for Forty Mile. He had barely made the turn when I lost sight of his headlamp in the blowing snow. This was going to be a long night and a long run. But the dogs just had 36 hours of rest and TLC, and they were screaming to hit the trail. Hugs, thanks, and high-5s, and I pulled the hook and we followed Jerry into the storm just before midnight, just a few minutes longer than our required 36-hour stay. Tanya later told me she stood and watched us drop onto the river and, in less than a few minutes, before we even made the turn, she lost sight of my headlamp in the darkness and swirling snow. She would post this to our Facebook page later that evening: "As they left together, the moon was trying to come out and the wind starting to die down a bit. Seeing 5 headlamps disappear down the Yukon River into a stormy night and hearing the howl of huskies echoing off the hills pulled everyone watching them back in time 100 years. Mushers and huskies vs the untamed Yukon..."

10

A Vision

While I was focused on trying to see the trail and the dogs, it was hopeless. Tanya and Ward went back to the campsite. Tanya went into the hot tent and said she stared in shock for a few seconds before hollering at Ward and bolting out of the tent carrying my insulated parka I wear under my suit. How could that have been missed! After staring at each other for a nanosecond, a team went past the campsite—Tamara, the last team to leave. Ward grabbed the coat and started running, catching up to her just as she had signed out and was about to pull her snow hook and head down onto the river. He told her how I had forgotten it and, graciously, she said, "Well, I can take it to him," then held onto it for a second looking at her sled as if trying to figure out how she could possibly fit it in anywhere. Like mine and every other musher's sled, hers was packed to the point of exploding. With Ward's help, they managed to bungie tie it under some gear she had packed on top of her sled. An hour or so later, when she caught up to me, she stopped and said, "I have something for you." I was baffled as to what it could be, as I hadn't even realized I had left it yet. I didn't know it then, but not having that jacket on later would have likely ended my race.

We continued north up the Yukon River. I ran with blind trust in Lily and Strider, as I couldn't see a thing. Much of that run I couldn't even see Jay and Zeus running in wheel, closest to the sled. Kyla and I would leap frog positions several times on that run, as we would stop to snack and check the dogs and the other would pass. Even though there were five teams out there in theory, always close together, it felt incredibly lonely in that storm, probably because I couldn't even see my dogs. At one point, the snow cleared for just an instant and I could see the whole team. I am not a really spiritual person, and I know it is going to sound crazy, but what I saw was that I had an extra dog. A dog was running in front of Lily and Strider. Lazer was there leading the team. The snow closed in around the dogs again, and I wouldn't see them again for some time until the trail veered west onto the Forty Mile River. At that point, I was back to 11 dogs on the line. When I tell that story, I often mention right away that it was likely sleep deprivation—mushers see crazy things sometimes when going on little sleep. But then Tanya reminds me that I had just slept over 12 hours in Dawson City, and I wasn't tired at that point. Some of my First Nation's friends ask me why I question what I saw, because they don't. I had had a dream about Lazer leading us through a storm, then he was in the video at the start of the banquet, then he was on the trail; maybe I don't need to question the vision anymore than that.

Lazer – one of my great first lead dogs

I thought I saw a light reflecting through the storm. While it was still blowing as we came to the Forty Mile Hospitality Stop, it was letting up some, for which I was grateful. All five teams arrived in Forty Mile within 20 minutes of each other—we were never far apart on the River coming in here at all.

Forty Mile is an old gold mine camp with the claim of being Yukon's oldest town, being founded when gold was discovered there in 1886. It was given its name as it was about 40 miles from Fort Reliance, an old trading post. Residents of Forty Mile today are working on restoring the camp. Sebastian was an awesome host. We had already met his wife Shelley, as she was one of the Quest race judges this year. He had a large cast iron pot with a fire going for hot water for the teams. After the team was bedded down and cared for, Sebastian gave us a quick tour of how they were fixing the place up. Tons of food waited for us too, and after the long night it was very welcome. None of us were in much of a hurry to get going after what we had run through, and, by waiting, the storm had let up.

Tamara was the first to leave, and the rest of us followed her within the next hour. I was scrambling because, at this point, I did not want to be the last one out, especially when I had never run this race before and we were heading into areas where there wouldn't be cabins or anyone to offer assistance if we got lost. Kyla and I left together with Didier following right after. It was around 4:30 and the sun was setting. We once again were going to be running during the dogs' favourite time of day as dusk descended.

Travelling along Forty Mile River was, without a doubt, the most beautiful place I have ever travelled with a team of dogs, and one of the most beautiful sights I had ever seen period. The way the mountains come down into the river and the mountains that form Top of The World Highway in the background are simply jaw-dropping. I found myself dreaming as we ran of coming back here one day with Tanya and the kids and trying our hand at panning for gold. Somewhere along there we also crossed the U.S.-Canada border, not that there was any major landmark to note that. The easiest border crossing I ever had!

As we ran through the night, it was wonderful to have a clear, starry sky again and I switched off my headlamp. Maverick caught the scent of something, and, knowing there were no checkpoints out here, I got a bit worried. Several miles later, though, we came across a tent and several teams were already there bedded down. We were close to American Summit. This tent was here for shelter not far from the base of the mountain.

It would make a good place to stop, and I bedded down the team and started the cooker for a nice hot meal. While it was clear again, the temperatures had also started to drop quickly. They say in this part of the Yukon River, you never get cold and wind together. It's always one or the other.

The dogs ate their hot soup happily and curled up to sleep. Kyla had pulled in behind us, and the crew was all here now with 6 teams camped out around the tent. Smoke billowed from the stove pipe sticking out the roof, and I looked forward to some warmth. I thought of how crowded it likely was and about sleeping in my sledbag that night. But it was getting so cold, I decided to go in. Lifting back the flap, I saw I was too late to the party; 4 sleeping bags were already stretched out on the floor, leaving no room for anyone else. I carefully stepped close to the small wood stove and sat down, almost hugging it for warmth. The heat made me instantly sleepy. Soon after I heard and felt the tent flap open and Kyla came in. "Oh, where are we going to sleep?" I said jump on top! She wiggled into her sleeping bag and turned around and jumped backwards, landing on top of everyone. No one even moved, and Kyla was soon asleep.

Kyla's launch had shifted everyone a little, and it wasn't long before I saw Jerry, who was along the outside wall, roll over and see me by the stove. He commented, "Here, I'll switch with you, you've got to get some sleep, too." I was really grateful and thanked him as we traded spots. Then I realized why Jerry had thought my spot sitting at the stove looked pretty good. His spot was half outside the tent wall from everyone squished in, and I was freezing in a matter of minutes as the cold air snuck in where the wall and floor material of the tent was gaping open. I lay there cursing for a while and then decided my sledbag would at least provide more shelter than where I was now. I got up and went outside again, getting into my sledbag. At least there was no snoring in my sled. I got a bit of sleep that night but not a very restful one.

American Summit would be our next challenge, and at an elevation of 3,400 feet, it was by a slight amount the smallest of the four main mountains we would go over on the race. The trail up American Summit is just a long, sweeping trail around the mountain. You just keep climbing; it was blustery but not crazy bad. As I climbed I would see the trail disappear and go around a bend and I would think I was almost to the top. Then as I round the bend, it just keeps going. The climb was similar to King Solomon Dome, and we went up around 2,000 feet.

I was the last one to start up American Summit, and when I got almost to the top, I ran into the American trailbreakers Mike and Daniel waiting for the last team to safely make it up. Mike warned me to keep running around the rim of the mountain rather than go into the bowl, even though it was the shorter way to the other side. He said if the wind picked up more it would become a blizzard in that bowl, and I would have a hard time finding my way out. As we ran around the rim as he suggested, I started noticing some strange lumps on the side of the trail. I assumed they were rocks and, as we went by one, I stuck out my ski pole to hit it and see what it was. I jumped when the second my ski pole hit it, a small Christmas tree exploded out of the snow. The weight of the hoar frost had bent them over, and then the snow and more frost just kept building up and weighing them down more. This was fun, and I hit the next one with my ski pole and watched a small tree explode up again. I kept doing this with silly childlike glee, chuckling each time it happened. I noticed the dogs glancing at me and what I was doing and then I stopped, thinking it was kind of childish doing this kind of shit. It was great fun for 15 minutes, though, and put a big grin on my face. Then I went back to poling with the dogs.

Eagle, I had been told, was a dry community, but as we started down the other side of the summit, there was what looked like a roadhouse that was closed up. I assumed it was outside town limits. Coming down American was a long 20-mile descent; not crazy steep, but you were definitely going down. The dogs had fun on this run, everyone except Gem. She started looking like she wasn't happy. I stopped the team and checked Gem, but I couldn't find anything wrong. I decided to let her ride in the sled for a while to see if that helped her.

I came into the village of Eagle as the sun was getting low in the sky and a young customs officer was waiting for me along with the checker, race judge, and veterinarian. He sternly told me he needed my passport and paperwork. I panicked, trying to remember if I had it with me and if so, where it was. I forgot that Tanya had carefully packed my passport and some cash in a Ziploc bag that was inside an inner pocket in my big parka. My face must have reflected my panic as the officer quickly laughed and said, "Don't worry about it. I was just joking with you. We already have all your paperwork from the Quest office."

The 3 stooges plus a few more were all there. Didier and I had our teams parked close together, and he mentioned he wasn't having fun anymore, that he might call it quits. We chatted as we cared for our teams, and I tried to tell him that the worst was behind us, and, as we had come this far, we couldn't quit now. I felt I had cheered him up and convinced him to keep going.

The people and hospitality in Eagle were amazing. This was the one checkpoint handlers couldn't get to, as the Top of the World Highway is closed in the winter, making Eagle a remote town even though in the summer you could drive here. The community centre was opened up for us, and there was incredible food everywhere, as well as a bed to sleep on. It was quite a welcome spot after a long 24 hours on the trail. Eagle was also the home of Wayne and Scarlett Hall, who had a touring kennel here. I enjoyed visiting with them and comparing notes on how we shared dogsledding with guests from around the world.

I laid down to sleep for a bit with sweet little Gemmy girl heavy on my mind. While all the dogs had passed their vet exams with no issues at all, Gem, the last 50 or so miles, just didn't look to be having fun anymore. During the Iditarod last year, as I had run into a First Nations elder coming into a remote village, he had asked me how my journey had been so far. I had replied it had been a good journey. He nodded and said, "Then the journey continues as long as it is a good journey, but when it is no longer a good journey for one of the dogs or for you, then the journey ends." Those words kept running through my head. If we had been in a checkpoint where the truck was, I wouldn't have thought twice about dropping Gem, knowing she would be with Tanya and Ward instantly. But if I dropped her here, she would watch us leave and then be flown to Central on a plane to meet up with Tanya and Ward.

I was still wrestling with the decision when I got up two hours later. The vet and vet tech knew what I was considering and assured me that if I left her here with them, they would baby her like their own dog and would be with her in the plane ride back to Central. I figured Tanya and Ward should be arriving soon in Central. They would have driven almost 2,000 kilometres all the way down to Whitehorse and then across to Alaska and back up to Circle, so Gem would be on the truck with them almost as soon as she got there. If I could have taken her in my sledbag, I would have, but with 160 miles to Circle, I needed to pack a ton of food again, and if I had another dog that needed to ride, there was no way I would have room for both. With the assurance again from the vet team, I signed the form to leave Gemmy with them, the hardest thing I've ever done.

We pulled out around 3:30 in the middle of the night. I gave Gem tons of cuddles before we left and talked to her, hoping she could somehow understand I would see her soon and she would see Tanya and Ward the next day. If she was a more outgoing dog, I would not have worried so much, but Gem was quiet and was my girl.

Didier was up, too. We were the last two teams there, and he assured me he would be following us and that I should get going; his dogs were faster and he would catch up. He definitely had faster dogs, and on the flat river running that we would be doing, I had no doubts he would catch us. I put my extra unneeded gear into a drop bag we had sent to this checkpoint, and, along with a $20 bill, left it with the checker to ship back to us. I packed the sled as full as I could and pulled the hook and we were on our way. I had stayed here too long already, delaying our departure because of Gem.

11

Shut Out

We pulled out of Eagle and made quite a ruckus. I didn't realize the trail would take us right through the Hall Family dog yard, and their dogs were quick to bark and howl a greeting to our dogs as we passed. We dropped down on the river headed for Circle, the dogs well rested and happy to be on the move again. It was a cold night but clear, and I found myself glancing backwards watching for Didier's headlamp as we ran.

Turns out Didier would leave Eagle as he said he would, but then he turned around and went back to Eagle and scratched. I now had the unwanted title of being last in the race, not that I would know it for a while, still thinking Didier was behind us.

This stretch would be 150 miles of pretty much all river running, and the dogs would get bored of it soon enough. While it was dark, it would not be too bad. But daybreak would show them nothing but endless river. As dawn was breaking, we arrived at the first hospitality stop of Trout Creek about 30 miles into the run, and we stopped here for our first good rest. I don't know the gentleman's last name, but Mike was his first name, and, while Eagle was his home, he spent a lot of time at his cabin here and welcomed mushers every year. He already knew about our team, as his daughter ran a team of Siberians in Eagle. Team bedded down and fed, I headed inside and was offered a bowl of moose stew and a place to catch a bit of sleep, which I gladly accepted for an hour. There was still no sign of Didier, and I was starting to think he wasn't coming, meaning I was in last place, and that worried me. Being in last hadn't worked out well last winter. Thanking Mike for his hospitality, we travelled on. The sun helped for sure, but it was still a cold day.

At dusk, another cabin had moose stew for me. I wasn't sure if it was Slaven's, but, as the trail passed right by, I saw a man outside on the river bank, so I stopped and asked him how much further it was to Slaven's, not wanting to presume it was Slaven's. He said it was up the trail another 20 miles or so. Then he said, "But I have some moose stew on, come on in and get warmed up!" I agreed, cared for the team, and then went in for a few minutes. A few minutes turned into an hour, and I said I had to get going, I was in a race. He argued with me, saying, "You can stay a little longer, who knows when the next person will come along this winter!" I obliged him and stayed in his warm cabin for another while but then told him I really had to get back on the trail. I wasn't gaining on the teams in front of me at this rate...

Slaven's only 20 miles away would be a short run. It was almost midnight already; I had stayed visiting with my new friend a lot longer than I had planned! The run over was uneventful, and it didn't take long to reach Slaven's. I cared for the dogs and, on another cold night, they all enjoyed the fresh straw and made their beds quickly and curled up as I cooked for them and cared for their feet. I figured Gem would be with Ward and Tanya this morning, and that made me relieved. Chores done, I headed towards the cabin. The smell of smoke from the woodstove was in the air and a welcoming light shone through the windows. Only problem was, there were only windows and no door. I circled the cabin several times, baffled as to how the hell you got in… I circled again—no door. This was crazy. I walked up to one of the windows and tapped on it, peering inside at everyone. I heard excited voices saying, "Someone is out there!" I heard a door open and someone called, "Around back, come around back." Turns out the door was behind a lean-to and, with no windows, it was so hard to see in the dark. Everyone got quite the laugh over my trying to figure out how to get inside.

Slaven's cabin was a blast—great people, great food, and a loft to sleep in as well. All our Dawson crew (with the exception of Didier) were here, and Johannes was with the group, too. We all had lots of laughs, and stories were flying. I laid down knowing the rest of them would be gone when I got up in a couple of hours, which was discouraging. It was good for the dogs to see other teams here, too.

One more run and we would be in Circle to meet up with Tanya, Ward, and the rest of the dogs. I was so looking forward to it. Sixty miles, and we would be off the Yukon River for good. Ten dogs and I pulled out of Slaven's a little after noon, having had a good 8-hour rest. It was a sunny, bright day but still cold. We had been warned this section of the race was usually the coldest.

Team members with Tanya and Ward waiting for us in Circle

I went into my snack bags for something to eat. While I normally don't enjoy greasy bacon any other time, when I am running and it is cold, I do crave fatty bacon. I pulled out the Ziploc with the bacon wrapped in foil in it. Over the years, as I have had dogs riding in the sledbag, when I take out the bacon they get to share some with me. Most of the dogs had ridden in the sled at some point, and they all seemed to know the exact sound of the bacon package. They loved bacon as much as I do, and now, when they hear the bacon wrapper, they start running while looking backwards, so I had two choices – 1) have the bacon out ahead of time so there was no wrapper to trigger them, or 2) share or we weren't going anywhere until the bacon was gone! Aster and Hosta in particular love bacon! All for one and one for all. Normally, I picked the sharing option.

The sun was setting, and I had never seen more beautiful warm light than in this area of the Yukon River even though it was so cold. The dogs picked up their pace as they usually do at the change of light, and I pulled out my headlamps. I heard a plane and looked up so see it dip its wings as it flew over me. I assumed it was flying from Eagle or Slaven's. Turned out Didier was on board, his dogs had already been flown out yesterday to Circle to his wife and handlers; now was the first they had a chance to get him out.

As we ran on into the night, I started thinking that I smelled smoke. Strange, as there were no cabins that I had seen that looked occupied. The smell got stronger... All of a sudden, I realized the smell was coming from me. I unzipped my outer parka quickly and saw smoke coming from my pocket. Pulling out my headlamp, batteries safely tucked in my inner pocket, we had a problem indeed. My headlamp batteries were on fire!

At this point, I heard a snowmobile approaching. I grabbed my backup headlamp so he would see me. Turned out it was George, the official photographer, who had been following the race since Whitehorse. He had purchased a new snowmobile for the trail but did not realize it didn't like the cold. Every day before he started out, he had to build a fire underneath his machine so it would warm up enough to start.

He pulled up beside me, asking if we were good. I said, well, our headlight batteries just caught fire, and we have a bit of a problem here. He chuckled and said good to hear it and kept going to Circle. I couldn't blame him; he sure didn't want to be stranded on the River with no way to get his machine running…

My GPS stopped working again, not because of me this time. Tanya and Ward were waiting for me in Circle but had no idea where I was. The plane landed and gave them an update. Then George arrived and told Tanya I wasn't far out and that I should be in within the hour.

I rounded a bend in the river and saw the lights of Circle in the distance. The northern lights were also putting on an amazing show, so I didn't need my headlamp anyway. I had a small one with me, too, but it was for working with the dogs and wouldn't do much to light up the trail. I started to notice a light on what I assumed was the river bank. It would stay in one spot focused on my direction for a bit and then disappear, but then would be back again. I started thinking it was a person, but who the hell would be out on this cold a night?

As the team and I reached Circle and ran up the bank, I realized the light I had seen was Tanya. She had been standing on the river bank watching for me and then gone in to quickly get warm before coming back out again. It was wonderful to see her, and we hugged as she quickly told me Gem was with them on the truck and happy. They had stopped in Central on the way into Circle to see who had been dropped. They told her it was Gem and that she was outside waiting for her and was just fine. Tanya went out and called, as she didn't see Gemmy. Instantly, out of a massive pile of straw, Gem's head popped up and, with a happy wag of her tail, was in Tanya's arms and back on the truck with the rest of her friends.

It was great seeing Kyla, Jerry, Tamara, and Johannes and their teams again, and I worked to get my team looked after as fast as possible. The dogs were all well bedded down here for what would turn out to be the coldest night of the race. I headed inside to find tons of food and the best sleeping spot in the fire hall, which also served as a jail, on top of the firetruck underneath the heater. That spot was taken, though, so the back room it was. I had no trouble falling asleep here!

The children of Circle made welcome signs for each musher

Coldest night of the race -60C a full moon shines on a trail marker

When I got up, everyone other than Johannes had left. I started getting ready. I also heard about overflow and the story of another musher who had come across really deep overflow on this next section and got himself in trouble. Thankfully, another musher had come along and helped him get a fire going and warmed up. Minus 60°C and overflow was not an exciting combination. The race judge handed me garbage bags to go inside my boots to hopefully keep my feet dry if I came across overflow. Mike said we would not. He had been on the river last night and it was fine then.

As dawn was breaking, we pulled the hooks and started down the trail to waterflow worries. Johannes was still at the checkpoint but was really sick. It didn't sound like he was going to be leaving. I worried something fierce on this whole run, waiting for overflow. It never came, but I can remember seeing the frozen tracks in the ice and snow where the musher had got into the deep overflow.

The best sleeping spot in Circle was on top of the firetruck by the heater

As it was, we were lucky. No overflow, and when we were past the worst section of the Birchy Creeks, I bedded down the team for a rest. I didn't realize we were only 20 miles from the checkpoint and everyone was watching my tracker, waiting for our arrival. Tanya told me she had been scared we were having problems with overflow and had gone to ask the race judge if that was the section of trail others had trouble in. The race judge and Mike looked at the GPS map carefully and Mike said, "No, he is fine, he is off the river now." That massively eased Tanya's mind. She was, however, standing outside waiting for us as we ran down the road and pulled into Central around 1:30 a.m. That just left the challenge of Eagle Summit.

There was someone else waiting for me in Central besides Tanya and Ward—Hans, the race marshal, and Dee, who was head of PR for the race, had also just arrived.

12

Legendary Eagle Summit

A hand shook me awake. Six a.m. I had asked for a wake-up call at this time, although more sleep would have been wonderful! Eagle Summit was ahead, the stretch of trail I had tried hard not to think about for the whole race, as it was known for being the hardest section of the 1,000-mile trail. Not just the steep climb up but also the wind and storms that hammered the summit. From Central, we would climb 2,700 feet to the Summit of Eagle and then drop down into Checkpoint 101. It was a deceivingly simple sounding 28-mile run until you looked at the elevation and started listening to stories of what happens on that summit. One year, the storm up there got so bad with teams stuck on top of the summit that air force black hawk helicopters were called in to land and rescue the teams. There were other stories of teams getting near the top only to spin around on their musher and come right back down the mountain, stories of teams camping out just below the treeline waiting for a storm to blow out or for their dogs to decide to try and climb again. Or teams tackling the summit together, taking turns up front leading to give the other team's dogs a rest.

I had no option to camp out and wait out any storms. We were already at the back of the race, so there was no one to take turns going up the mountain with, or dogs in front of ours to inspire our team to chase them up. It was just us. But I had Lily as an incredibly driven lead dog and an amazing team of dogs behind her.

I pulled on my suit and boots. Sitting there thinking the worst wasn't going to get us any closer to Fairbanks or put the mountain at our backs. I asked the volunteer to have the veterinarian come and check Strider again for me.

The race marshal last night had come in to tell the four of us that we had to be running towards the summit by 8 a.m. to beat a storm that was coming in. If we didn't get over Eagle before the storm hit ,we wouldn't get over it and finish the race.

The dogs stirred as I got close to them. Some got up and shook and redug their beds, settling down again as I served up another meal. Tanya was waiting near the back of the sled and we chatted about the trail ahead as I fed the dogs and started repacking the sled. She said at the moment, the trail was supposed to be fine, and while a storm was coming, I should be over the summit before it hit. A veterinarian came over to check Strider. I had already pretty much made up my mind that he would stay here. While I had no doubt he wanted to go with us and would give his all, the last thing we needed was to have to put him in the sled part way up Eagle Summit and have another 50 lbs. to pull over the mountain. But, more importantly, he always gave his all, and if he already wasn't feeling good, that was not going to be in his best interest. No matter how much I wanted him up front with me for that climb, the best decision for Strider was to leave him here with Tanya and Ward.

Central Corner Roadhouse

The veterinarian agreed, and we signed the paperwork that Strider would stay with Tanya and Ward. To say Strider did not agree with my decision was an understatement. He flat out refused to stand up and walk with Ward as he came over with the leash, and Strider adored Ward. He flattened himself on the ground as much as he could. Ward had to pick him up and carry him to the truck, all the while Strider looking over Ward's shoulder at me. The look in his eyes broke my heart, and I had a lump in my throat. I had to remind myself it was in his best interests to go with Tanya and Ward. Glory knows it wasn't in my best interest or the teams'. I had counted on him leading beside Lily up the summit. Between the two of them, I had no doubt that we could reach the top one way or another, but now that left Lily leading on her own. God knows she is more than capable of leading on her own, but this was going to be one of the most challenging sections of trail we had ever run, and having Strider beside her shouldering the responsibility of leading would have helped her.

It was time to go. I packed the rest of the gear into the sled and zipped it up and headed into the checkpoint to thank everyone and grab one last quick sip of coffee and to check on the latest trail condition report. I was told the summit at the moment was calm, so a good time to climb, but a storm was brewing, so get up and over sooner than later. There was also a report of some overflow a little ways out of the checkpoint before we started to climb. Nothing serious, I was told, just a spot where glaciated ice keeps flowing and building up.

With thanks and wishes of good luck for the climb, I closed the door behind me and headed to the team. With booties on the dogs, a hug from Tanya, and "See you on the other side" from Ward, we were off. The trail followed the road for a bit before weaving through the trees. It was deceptively flat, and the dogs felt it was like the trails back home and were having fun with the twisting trails. Then we reached the overflow… It was crazy; sled runner tracks literally went right into and disappeared into a massive block of glare ice 4 feet high. My tired mind grappled with how it was even possible. The ice had grown a ton since the last teams had passed. There was no way we could climb over that, so we had to work our way through the trees to get around the ice. It was heavily treed in this section of trail, and the edge of the trail had been pushed in so I didn't have much room to work with. It took likely an hour as we carefully moved the team around the glaciated ice. I would work a bunch of dogs through the trees, get some slack, work another bunch of dogs through, get the sled that was jammed between trees unstuck and move ahead, and then start all over again. It was tiresome and frustrating, both for the dogs and me. Thank goodness it was this late in the race, when they were willing to be patient, and not at the start when they would never have stood still and waited for me to sort things out.

Shortly after getting back on the trail, we started to climb. The trail was good to start with, and we were still protected by the treeline. Ahead, though, I saw the end of the treeline as we approached. I stopped to give the dogs a rest and a snack. You could see it was blowing like hell beyond the shelter of the trees. Lily in single lead was the first to step out into the open above the treeline of Eagle as we started moving again. I watched helplessly as the wind hit her from the side so hard it knocked her off her feet and rolled her over. But that amazing girl got back onto her feet and crouching lower, moving ahead as the whole team left behind the shelter of the treeline. As the wind knocked Lily over again, I went up beside her and hooked myself into the gangline. Slowly but surely, we were climbing. We slowed for a break again and noticed Jay; unbelievably, he was bracing himself. The rest of the dogs laid down for a break to get out of the wind. But Jay, that incredible big, fluffy wheel dog, would go to work. His tug would be slack as the team was climbing, but the second he felt us slowing down, I would watch in amazement as he started to brace himself. Placing his feet so he was in a stance of utter strength, he lowered his head and I saw all his muscles tense up as he started to brace himself. While the team laid down to rest, he stood strong and held the sled in place, keeping it from pulling the team backwards down the mountain. He stood like that, holding the sled stationary on his own, until Lily and I started getting up and the rest of the dogs would quickly get up with us and start moving forward again. Then Jay would just walk, not pulling, taking his breather then as the rest of the team did the work moving us up the mountain. Jay was 7 years old. He had never been on a mountain like this in his life. How the hell did he know to hold the sled from carrying us back down the mountain? Moments like this made me realize the sheer brilliance of these dogs. Jay might not be a lead dog, but he was my rock climbing that mountain.

Jay frosted up from Eagle Summit

Part way up the first section while we were having a break, the trail swept Mike and Daniel past us on their snowmobiles. The team and I were catching a breather, and I was having a smoke. Mike thought that was hilarious, that I would smoke when needing to catch my breath, and has told me since that he tells all rookies that if Hank can get up Eagle puffing on a cigarette, you can certainly climb it! As I watched them go up the mountain, a gust of wind grabbed the heavy freight toboggan. They were pulling with all their trail gear and ripped it right off the hitch of the snowmobile and flipped it. It took both of them a huge effort to get it flipped back over, hooked to the sled, reloaded, and continue up the mountain. On Eagle, there was nowhere to hide from the wind. It looked as bare as the moon, only white with snow.

We hit the saddle of the summit, and the worst part was ahead, the steepest part. But, on the plus side, we were now sheltered from the wind a bit as we turned into the saddle. I would need to help the team on this section by pushing the sled. I unsnapped Maverick and brought him up beside Lily to help her climb, face the wind, and keep the team moving up. Maverick was young, big and strong, but brawn isn't what it is all about, for sure. Maverick thought it was just stupid to go up the saddle and would have been more than happy spinning us around and heading right on back down that mountain, but Gramma Lily quickly let him know that wasn't an option and he quickly gave up that notion and took her lead, putting his head down to climb. As we neared the top of the saddle, the trailsweeps were sitting on top, and Mike snapped a quick picture of us nearing the summit; all of us, including me, heads down, working hard. Several minutes later, we reached the top. The worst was behind us, and we stopped for a good rest and snack as the trailsweeps carried on to the checkpoint. The remaining few miles into the check point were gradual downhill, and the team seemed to know the feat they had just accomplished. As we headed into Mile 101 checkpoint, Maverick picked up the scent of the checkpoint and got everyone all fired up. Between going downhill and the smell of the bacon ahead, they looked like they were on fire with tails all up and bushed out, ears up, and running like they had just started the race. Tanya snapped a picture as we rounded the corner in the trail that brought us into Mile 101, and the dogs looked like they had conquered the world! While only a 28-mile run, it had taken us close to 7 hours.

*Almost to the top of Eagle Summit, Lily & Maverick
in lead as I push the sled*

On this side of the summit sitting in Mile 101, it was a lovely day; no wind and sunny. Long time checkpoint manager Peter welcomed us and got us signed in. Our drop bags were all sitting in a toboggan waiting for me, thanks to the volunteers. I grabbed the bale of straw and spread it out quickly for the dogs to snuggle down into. The sun here was so warm, though, most just laid on top without burrowing down in as they munched on their chunks of frozen salmon while waiting for their main meal to cook. I worked from front to back, taking their booties off, massaging feet and shoulders. Tanya and Ward were waiting for us and told me Strider was doing better, although would have still rather been with me and the team—I had no doubt. They had parked the truck likely close to a kilometre away from the checkpoint so Strider wouldn't see or hear us and vice versa. After the team had wolfed down their warm soup, they quickly settled in for a good sleep. They knew the routine well now and didn't waste time or energy when dinner was done before curling up and sleeping.

Team settingly down for a rest at 101

Dogs cared for and snoozing, I headed towards one of several small cabins that had smoke curling out of the chimney. As I opened the door, a wall of heat hit me—and the delicious smell of bacon! Again, I would eat and be treated like a king in a tiny remote cabin in the middle of Alaska by people who volunteered every year to care for the teams that cross this remote old mining camp known simply as Mile 101 (as it is about 101 miles from Fairbanks on the Steese Highway). When I could not have eaten another bite if I tried, Peter led me to the sleeping cabin again. It was toasty warm, and I really didn't need a sleeping bag at all. I don't even remember lying down after taking my boots and suit off, and it only seemed like minutes later, rather than the 2 hours I had asked to sleep, when Peter was shaking me awake with the message that a hot coffee and energy drink awaited—and more bacon before we headed down the trail to Rosebud Summit.

101 Checkpoint

Feeding the team in the warm sun of 101

13

The Wildest Ride of My LIfe

I was so damned tired. I sat up, trying to get my brain to catch up as I pulled my suit and boots on. Stepping out from the dark cabin, the brightness of the beautiful afternoon sun blinded me for several seconds. I stumbled my way to the other cabin to grab the promised coffee. I wondered how much coffee I had drunk since Whitehorse. I always loved coffee and drank more than I should, but the last 11 days, it seemed like my coffee consumption had hit an all-time high. Sitting down with Tanya, I scarfed down a bit more food, but I wasn't that hungry. I had just eaten a couple of hours ago. I wouldn't find out until the next day that, in fact, it was much sooner than I realized, and my two hours of sleep had been reduced to only one hour.

Right after I had gone to the bunkhouse, Peter and Mike had come to Tanya and asked her to come with them for a minute. From outside the cookhouse, they pointed up to Rosebud Summit. Peter asked her if she saw the eddies swirling on top of the mountain. She did. Mike told her it meant that in a very short period of time, that mountain would be a whiteout with dangerous winds. He said the trail crew were leaving shortly and once they were over the mountain and the storm hit, no team would be able to make it to the other side. Either Hank and the team left now, or they wouldn't finish. Tanya understood but also knew how exhausted I was. She had looked at Peter and said, "I'm glad it is you waking him up after an hour of sleep and not me!" Peter laughed, saying he'd tell him coffee and his energy drinks were waiting for me. Smiling, he headed to wake me up without mentioning any of this to me.

The dogs were happy; the warm afternoon sun had allowed them a very comfortable sleep, and they stood and shook as I approached. I got their meal ready and most ate well as I started repacking the sled. Mike and Peter came over and explained about the storm rolling in and that we had to get over that mountain as quickly as we could. Mike and Daniel would be ahead of me but wouldn't be waiting. They were understandably anxious to get to the safety of the other side of the summit before things got bad. Mike told me if I didn't get across before the winds hit, they would slam the team and me hard. He mentioned a rock outcropping where we could get some shelter from the storm if need be, but again, he calmly emphasized getting over that mountain as fast as we could. As I bootied the dogs, they fired up their snowmobiles, and, with a wave, headed out.

Putting booties on dogs as we get ready to leave 101 as the sun sets

I was nervous. No one ever really talked about Rosebud, so I hadn't really given it much thought. Everyone always talks about Eagle Summit, but Mike hadn't mentioned Eagle's winds to us at all, meaning what we were about to face was likely going to be worse than what we had just come through. Once again, I found myself wishing Strider was still up in lead with Lily. But Maverick, partially thanks to his grandmother Lily giving him some flack, had done well helping to get us over Eagle.

Giving Tanya a hug as she said "see you in Two Rivers later tonight", Ward a high 5 and a thank you to all the amazing folks at 101 who made a tiny little dot on the map such a wonderful place, I took the clipboard from Peter and officially signed out of 101 at 4:30 pm. Pulling the snowhook and whistling to the team, we left the sanctuary of 101 behind.

Last team out of 101, headed to Rosebud Summit

The first section of trail was flat and easy running as the dogs got warmed up and into the travelling groove. They weren't used to getting up off their straw with that short of a nap. The trail wound across the road and along a river bed (gold country). Out of no where, about a dozen caribou were suddenly running in front of the team, let me tell you we went from getting into a nice pace to full out hunt mode in 1 second flat and anyone watching our tracker I'm sure were thinking we were running down one heck of a hill at the speeds we hit. The caribou headed in a different direction though, not caring to stick to marked trails and the team lost interest in the chase and continued down the trail.

We started to climb It wasn't as bad as Eagle, thankfully, and the dogs, having just rested, were happy running through the wooded trail as we wound our way up. The caribou had been a blessing, as they were all in hunt mode now, searching for any other caribou that might make for a fun chase.

We were finally at the top, and I was thankful we seemed to have beaten the worst of the wind. It was blowing, but Eagle had been worse. The top of the summit was likely 10 miles across, and, as we approached what was likely the halfway mark, our luck changed. The wind started howling and it felt like I had just been punched by a fist, the wind hit us so hard. I saw the rock outcropping that Mike had mentioned, but my goal was to get us all off this mountain as fast as possible. I sure didn't want us pinned down up here for hours or a day in a blizzard.

Lily put her head down into the wind, as did Maverick, and we slowly made progress towards what looked like a drop off. Upon getting to the far side of the summit, I realized with a knot in my stomach it was in fact a drop off. Again, no one had mentioned how steep the descent off Rosebud was, and dark was falling fast. Camping in this storm to do the run in the daylight was not an option, so I dug threw my sledbag and pulled out drop chains. Stopping the team, I hooked them down and pulled out a snack bag. They all happily accepted a chunk of frozen steak and laid down to munch it while I flipped my sled on its side to wrap the chains around one runner, and then did the same with the other runner.

Roughlocking, they called it, and the only other time I had done it was when freezing rain had made the trail so slippery when I was running at home. I had never run a descent before on which I felt I needed to do this.

I wish I knew how to put into words what that run down the backside of the mountain was like. It was dark now, so I was using my headlamp to see the dogs and the trail and trail markers. Even with my weight alternating between the drag mat, the runners, and bracing off the ground to steer the sled, we went down at a crazy speed. The storm clouds blocked out all light the stars might have shed, and it was pitch black. My headlamp was bouncing light off the reflectors on the trail markers, which, with our rapid descent, looked like floating lights in the night sky. It was a surreal experience, and my adrenaline was pumping insanely as we plunged down the mountain. I had never been so happy to hit the bottom of a mountain or hill in my life. From the dog's point of view, they looked like they had had a blast, flying down the mountain, and were all smiles with tails flying high. In their minds, it had been a fun, fast run.

I hooked down to take the chains off my runners and check all the dogs, making sure no one had twisted a wrist or shoulder on that wild ride. I need not have worried. Tails were all wagging, tongues out, they were one happy bunch of dogs. I could almost feel them looking at me wondering, "What were you so worried about back there?"

The checkpoint of Two Rivers should only be about 15 miles in front of us, I thought, and, if I was right, Maverick's nose would pick it up in about another 5 miles, rallying the team that a checkpoint and lots of awesome people were just up the trail. Giving each one of them a pet, I said, "Ok, you clowns, let's get going to Two Rivers" and headed back to the sled and pulled the hook. Indeed, about 45 minutes later, Maverick's nose went up a bit, ears focused straight ahead, and his tail went up a little higher—he had picked up the scent of the checkpoint. About an hour later, as we ran down a slight grade, the trail curved around a hill and, as I felt the team pick up speed as the sled rounded the bend, the lights of what I assumed was Two Rivers were less than a kilometre away. It was still pitch black, but I turned around anyway, knowing that Rosebud and Eagle Summits were now behind us. The team had conquered the hardest sections of the Yukon Quest.

Now, with rest at Two Rivers, we were less than a hundred miles to the finish line in Fairbanks, and it was all pretty much flat trails and river running. By the time night fell again, we would be Yukon Quest finishers. And with that thought and so much pride for these dogs running through me, I felt I would burst. Lily and Maverick brought us into Two Rivers and a mandatory 8-hour rest.

Jester rests in Two Rivers

14

The Red Lantern's Glow

Red Lanterns are more than just an antique warm beckoning light in the mushing world. During the gold rush days, roadhouses would be found every 50 miles—the average daily travel distance by dogteam/horse. As dusk approached, the roadhouse would light the red lantern hanging outside their door to show the way and welcome teams still not in for the night. The light would stay burning until the last expected team arrived. Today, long-distance races still use the red lantern to signify when the last team is safely off the trail and the race concludes for another year. The red lantern award is the least coveted of all awards, as it is given to the last team to finish the race, but it also symbolizes the determination to cross the finish line. If you are going to be near the back of the pack, might as well have an award! Over the years, there have been mushers that, knowing they would be one of the last to finish, have tried to outsmart their competitors to end up being the last across the finish line. Brian Donaghue is the only musher in history to hold Red Lanterns from both the Yukon Quest and the Iditarod.

There was no one else to worry about trying to stay behind to get the Red Lantern in this year's Quest, though. As the team and I left the last checkpoint of Two Rivers after a good sleep headed to Fairbanks, there were only three other teams left on the trail, and Tamara, Kyla, and Jerry were all at least 6 hours ahead of me. The morning dawned, snowing heavily, with about three inches of fresh snow having fallen since we arrived the previous night. Lily wasn't very keen to head out, but Maverick was in good spirits, and once we ploughed through the unpacked checkpoint area to the harder trail underneath the snow, she got in a happier mood. It wasn't cold, which was wonderful after the last five days. This 77-mile run was all pretty flat, on trails used by local mushers and river beds. I was looking forward to this run and figured the dogs would enjoy it, too, with lots of activity and forested trails like back home.

Military volunteers at Two Rivers giving our dropped dogs some TLC

Approximately 20 miles into the run, the trail crossed a main road. The Two Rivers volunteers warned it might not be manned now, so Tanya and Ward were going to be there to make sure the team got safely across. They made sure to park the truck a ways from the crossing so the dogs wouldn't think it was time to get back on the truck and the run was over.

Approaching a road crossing, 40 miles to the finish line

Before we crossed the road, I stopped to snack the dogs. Everyone was running great, and, of course, upon seeing Tanya and Ward again so soon, all tails and ears perked up. Plus, they could smell other houses and dogs, so I think they knew we were nearing the end of the race. I asked Tanya how much further we had to go, and she said the store down the road had told them it was about 45-50 miles from the finish line. A 6 to 7-hour run. With the dogs excited to keep going, I bid Tanya and Ward farewell and pulled the hook. Tanya called out as we pulled away, "See you at the finish line!" The Finishers Banquet was that night. Normally, it would be the Saturday night, but a conflict with the hotel had required the change to the Friday night. Tanya and Ward had tickets, and we were expected to cross the finish line in time to go. Not high on my list of things to do the second after stepping off a sled after a 1,000-mile journey, but rules said all mushers across the finish line before the banquet started must attend. We planned to be in Fairbanks just before the banquet kicked off.

Tanya and Ward would stay there for an hour or two and do what fellow veteran handler Sue Ellis termed "dog truck vomit." After almost two weeks on the road following a Quest team, dog trucks became a disaster, with leftover drop bags chucked anywhere there was room, gear, garbage, harnesses, booties, etc. Before there would be room in the truck again for the dogs and me, a massive reorganization would have to take place. At least the day had turned lovely, making the task more bearable. Tanya later told me they had Loretto, Howler, Strider, Gem, Jed, Blitz, and Andy all out around the truck as they worked, and the dogs had enjoyed some snacks and stretching out in the sun. Upon throwing another piece of salmon the dogs' way, Ward had said, "I think they have all gained 5 pounds while travelling with us. Hank is going to think they are all fat!"

Finally, with every cooler, bag, and piece of gear on the ground around the truck, things started to take shape, with all leftover meat packed back away in coolers, all part bags of kibble combined together and packed in another section of the truck. All used (and frozen) booties in one massive garbage bag and stuffed into one of the dog boxes. Old straw was pulled out of all the dog beds and a brand-new bale of lovely straw broke apart to make fresh, deep, warm beds for each of the dogs when they arrived in Fairbanks that night. Salmon was left out and put in the truck to thaw so each dog would get a lovely thawed salmon steak once across the finish line. The truck was ready for us.

Snack time – steak strips

The next 10 or so miles were exciting for the dogs, running past stores, other teams, and down trails that had forks that went off into mushers' kennels before we came down onto the river. Like many rivers in Alaska, the Chena river meanders as it has cut its way through the land over centuries. While we might have only been 30 miles from Fairbanks, it turned out to seem—and maybe be—a hell of a lot further on that river.

The sun was starting to set, and we ran onwards towards the finish line. Problem was, I was no longer seeing trail markers. I didn't think there was any way we had gotten off the trail, and this trail was a well packed one, but still, markers wouldn't just blow over or away on a sheltered river like this. I started questioning whether we were on the right trail. Imagine that—less than 40 miles from the bloody finish line and getting lost! My uncertainty translated to the team, and Lily started taking us up trails that led off the river only to end up in someone's back yard or in someone's kennel and realize that couldn't be right, and then we'd have to turn around and retrace our steps. Nothing discourages a dogteam more than having to turn around and go back the way they just came...and we did this over and over and over. I was beyond discouraged. I was getting frustrated and angry, as were the dogs, and each time we had to turn around, everyone's tempers were flaring. Uncertainty does that to a team.

Dusk was now upon us, and still, as I swung my headlamp around from side to side in search of the telltale reflective light off the trail markers, my light just went into the dark, picking up nothing. We had travelled over 900 miles through the Yukon and Alaskan wilderness with trailmarkers hidden in blizzards, knocked over from high winds on mountain tops, and still we had not had this much issue being sure we were on track. Now, with literally dozens of trails/tracks running off and on the river, I was really getting worried. One thing to get turned around in the middle of nowhere, but with folks watching my tracker to see us cross the finish line, that just created more stress!

As we came around yet another bend in the river, I noticed a bonfire in the distance. Hopefully, they would be able to at least let me know if we were on the right trail. As we got closer, the dogs' ears were all pointing forward, listening to the voices. Their tails went up higher as they always do when we approached people, and their trot quickened. I saw a small girl run out from the fire towards us holding what looked like batons that you see at airports that runway crews carry and use to direct jets into terminals. She was waving them as if to beckon the team and me into their campfire. It was such a sweet sight, and she reminded me of Michaela and Jessica who were at home likely watching the tracker to see us cross the finish line.

About a dozen people were around the fire, I noted, as I stopped the team and sunk the snowhook. I asked them if we were on the right trail to the finish line, and they assured me we were. They said we were about 20 miles from the Finish Line. I had only heard 20 miles for two hours… Turned out they were all members from the Eielson Air Force Base and had been following the teams' progress and came out to cheer us on. They even had a coffee for me, best coffee I've ever tasted. Feeling my spirits buoyed that we were on the correct trail and not far from the finish line, I thanked them and bent to pull the snowhook to cheers of good luck and congratulations. A man stepped forward and said, "Sir, do you have a free hand?" I said sure, and he reached out and placed something in my mitt. I thanked him and slipped it into my pocket. On the plus side, there wasn't any doubt we were going to miss the banquet.

What I didn't know was that our online community as well as Yukon Quest fans from around the world were all on that last run with the team and me. Had I known that, it would certainly have changed my feeling of being so alone on the trail that night, as everyone else was sitting down at the banquet celebrating the race, volunteers, mushers, and dogs. Knowing I had so much company in spirit would have made that run a lot more enjoyable. Tanya and Ward were waiting for us, having checked into a hotel right by the finish line. Tanya was watching every step of our progress through the online tracker and posting to our growing Facebook community. She explained about the Red Lantern, and, as the team and I travelled the last hour of our 1,000-mile journey, the live webcam at the finish line couldn't accommodate all the viewers trying to get in to watch. People started posting to Tanya from around the world that they had red lanterns or red candles lit in their windows for the team. Tanya still gets emotional when we speak, retelling how people around the world from Australia to England from Haliburton to South Africa posted they had candles and lanterns lit and glowing in their windows for the team that night as we finished our journey.

Yukon Quest Fairbanks finish line at sunset as the team and I got closer

The glow from the lights in Fairbanks got steadily brighter and, finally, we were running down the river through the city. We turned yet another bend, and before the sled and I were around the corner, I knew from the dogs' change in pace and attitude we were there. Seconds later, I saw what they saw—lights on the river aimed on the Yukon Quest Finish Line banner and people waiting for us. Turned out we totally missed the banquet, and some of the other mushers, vets, volunteers, and fans had come from the banquet to cheer us across the finish line. It was a far bigger crowd of people than I was anticipating, to say the least!

Lily, maybe sensing my lack of excitement with a crowd of people, or maybe since, like me, she wasn't a real people kind of dog, decided we were not going to run into that group of people. She picked one of many snowmobile trails that would take us around the excitement and keep us going right on down the river. As we started to veer away from the fencing that would lead us to the finish line, I saw Tanya break away from the crowd and head in Lily's direction. A quick reassuring pat and word, and Tanya led Lily towards the lights. And with that, our 10-year dream and journey to finish a 1,000-mile race was complete. With my headlamp shining behind them, Lily and the team ran under the finish line and cameras went off, celebrating the finish of the 2011 Yukon Quest. All teams were now safely home and off the trail.

You would think I would have felt elated. I thought I would have, but in truth, I was exhausted and in a foul mood from the frustration of the run and no trail markers for miles. After hugging each dog, Tanya reached me with a hug and quickly picked up on my mood. In my ear, she whispered, "There are lots of people here to welcome you and also interview you and get photos, please smile just for a few minutes."

Marti Steuri came over to me holding the beautiful Red Lantern, donated by the Whitepass Railway. While it was meant to be a symbolic lantern, Marti and another spectator had figured out how to get a bit of oil into it so it would light. They had me blow out the flame, officially ending the 2011 Yukon Quest. I got through an interview or two with media, hugs, and congratulations from volunteers, veterinarians, and race officials, and also mushers Brent Sass, Mike Ellis, and Lance Mackey and others who had come down after the awards banquet to welcome us off the trail.

Crossing the finish line with my headlamp shining the way

Ward mentioned the truck was just up the river bank, and with a final thanks to everyone (and a good chug of Bailey's) I pulled my snowhook for the last time on this journey and the team, with Ward running in front of us, headed to the truck. Ward and Tanya had a big piece of fresh unthawed salmon waiting for each of the dogs, and they wolved them down; even Jay, who would not eat frozen salmon, was delighted with the big thawed piece. One by one we took their booties off and unharnessed them and lifted them into their beds in the truck as each took great joy at digging into the mound of fresh straw to make their beds just perfect for the night. It was wonderful to see Strider, Andy, Gem, Loretto, Howler, Blitz, and Jed again, who all gave us big howls, tail wags, and paws as I hugged each in turn. I so wished that each of them had crossed that finish line with us. They had all been vital parts of this team and deserved that.

Finally, sled loaded into the back of the truck just as it was, bowls, harnesses, booties, and everything else picked up, I got into the truck. We drove the two blocks to the hotel, and, as we got out and peaked in on each dog, they were all curled up, asleep already. Now it was my turn. I don't remember much from then until the next morning, but Tanya tells me I walked into the hotel room and fell forward like a stiff board onto the bed in all my winter gear—boots, snowsuit and all—and didn't move for three hours, and then stirred just long enough to get my winter gear off and get into bed before not stirring for another 10 hours.

*The glowing red lantern handed to me to blow out
and officially end the race*

I woke completely disoriented. I had no idea where I was. Worse, no one was there to ask. I left the room and headed to the lobby, but no one I knew was there, either. No Tanya or Ward. I headed outside—no dog truck. I was starting to panic as it just dawned on me I had no phone, wallet, ID, or even money. I realized the Yukon Quest office was right across the street, so I headed there only to be welcomed by Marti. Taking one look at me, she quickly must have realized I was still a sleep-deprived musher and was quick to tell me my truck was across the river in a parking lot where it was when we finished last night, and Tanya and Ward were looking after the dogs.

She gave me a hug and, thanking her, I headed over. The dogs saw me coming and gave me a rowdy welcome. You would never know by looking at them that they had just finished a 1,000-mile journey. They looked ready to see where we were off to next! But the next journey was our 5,000-mile drive to Haliburton. It was time to go home.

We returned to the hotel to pack up, and, as I picked up my Cabella's suit, I remembered the man from the campfire the night before handing me something. "Someone gave me something last night," I mumbled as I dug through all the pockets stuffed with hand warmer packages and old warmers, booties, batteries, and all kinds of odds and ends after 1,000 miles of wilderness. I felt something round and smooth and pulled out a beautiful coin. On the one side read "Challenge Coin," on the other side "Eisenhour Air Force Base, Passing Gas and Freezing Ass." I was speechless; the soldier last night had given me, a complete stranger, his challenge coin.

Tanya posted it on Facebook, hoping we would find out who had shared this random act of kindness. As I was reading the incredible number of kind and touching messages sent to us over the last 24 hours, a message came in about the coin. The soldier's name was Lee Watros, and he shared that watching the team the last few days travelling through the blizzards on mountains and behind the rest of the teams had inspired him, and they decided to build a bonfire to welcome us as we travelled to the finish line. He had wanted to give me something. He felt the challenge coin he had earned was an appropriate gift for what the team and I had accomplished.

With hugs and goodbyes said, that story and the coin packed safely in the truck, dogs snuggled down in their beds and Tanya dropped off at the Fairbanks airport to fly back to Ontario to be home with the kids as quickly as possible, we pulled out of Fairbanks headed for home.

To this day, I have not met Lee Watros in person, but his coin, along with the Yukon Quest 2011 Red Lantern, are two of my most prized possessions, and both get shared with every audience we speak to.

It was just starting to sink in that the team had done it, we had finished the Yukon Quest. I was bursting with pride in each and every one of my dogs, what they had done, what we had conquered, and the journey that was now behind us. In less than two weeks' time, the Yukon Quest had made us part of their family. Some of our best friends in the world were made along that trail, not to mention memories that I will treasure for all my days. But, while I knew we would all be back at the Yukon Quest again, what kept running through my mind as each mile took us closer to Haliburton was the next journey the dogs and I would head out on. We still had unfinished business with the Iditarod trail.

The Yukon Quest finish line

Glossary

- **Bootie** – cloth material that slips over the dogs' paws to protect them, elastic Velcro on the top to keep them in place

- **Brake** – piece of metal at the back of the sled that a musher steps on to slow/stop the team

- **Capillary Refill** – When you push on the dogs gum until it goes white and then watch how fast it turns pink again to assess the circulatory health of the dog

- **Checkpoint manager** – looks after all logistics, from volunteers to required equipment, food, technology, etc., at their checkpoint

- **Cooker** – a steel pail with holes cut in the side for draft. A small pan sits in the bottom of the pail for fuel and then a pot sits on top of that to hold the snow that the fuel will melt into water to cook a hot soup for the dogs

- **Drag mat** – normally a piece of rigged plastic snowmobile track that is at the back of the sled and a musher can stand on to slow the pace of the team by resistance

- **Dog coat** – the dogs wear these and they Velcro over their chest and under their belly to keep them warmer, fleece on the inside, a water resistant material on the outside

- **Dropbag** – a large grain sack that all the supplies you need on a race are shipped in

- **Drop chain** – like a small leash but a chain with a snap on each end so a dog can quickly be tied to anything safely

- **Dropped dog** – a dog that is left with handlers or veterinarians at a checkpoint instead of going on with the team

- **Excavator** – a large machine with a big scoop on the front used for digging up ground

- **Iditarod** – 1,000-mile dogsled race across Alaska

- **Jumble ice** – when river's ice breaks up and drifts around and then refreezes so the ice is frozen in chunks making for a very rough trail; sometimes chainsaws are used to try to cut out a smoother trail through the jumble ice

- **Gangline** – the rope that all the dogs are attached to and that then attaches to the sled

- **Gee** – turn right

- **Haw** – turn left

- **Hoar frost** - refers to white ice crystals deposited on all exposed objects, sometimes just a fine layer but also can be several centimeters thick

- **Hydro line** – a large cleared swath through Algonquin Park where power line towers run through that has a rough utility road and is also used as a snowmobile trail in the winter

- **Lead dog** – dog(s) that run at the front of the team

- **Magic carpet ride** – when everything goes as perfect as it possibly can for a musher and team

- **Neckline** - the line that runs from the gangline to the dogs' collars

- **Overflow** – water that runs off mountains and stays on the top of ice, creating the illusion of a frozen lake or river when in fact it is not. The ice is still safe underneath the water lying on top of it

- **Plastic** – the small strips that are on the bottom of the sled runners to help the sled slide over snow and ice. Different colours work better for various temperatures and conditions

- **Race judge** – each checkpoint has a race judge that works with the race marshal

- **Race marshal** – from the time the first team leaves the starting line, the race marshal is in charge of all decisions that need to be made for the race

- **Racket strap** – A fastener used to hold down cargo or equipment during transport. Normally made up of heavy webbing and a device to tighten that webbing around what it is holding

- **Seney 300** – 300-mile race in Michigan that is a qualifying race for Iditarod and Yukon Quest

- **Sledbag** – the heavy duty cloth bag custom-made to fit inside the sled; has a heavy duty zipper on the top to keep all items packed in the sled secured

- **Skid** – a wood pallet that is used for shipping items

- **Snowhook** – piece of metal that has two prongs that act like an anchor for a dogsled, put into the snow to hold a team in place

- **Snubline** – a piece of rope attached to the sled that a musher will tie off to a tree for added security to keep a team in place

- **Stakeout** – how line dogs are snapped to when they stop to get out and stretch, eat, and drink while traveling so they are safe, usually attached to a truck or trailer for security

- **Switchback** – when a trail is too steep to climb straight up so it goes up a mountain from side to side. You go one direction and make a sharp turn to head in the other direction, gradually working your way to the top

- **Team dog** – dogs that run in the middle of the team

- **Trail sweeps** – the people on snowmobiles that stay at the back of the race to pick up trail markers, deal with trail issues, and make sure everything is ok with mushers at the back of the race

- **Treeline** – the point on a mountain where elevation gets so high and no trees grow

- **Tug** – the line that runs from the dog's harness to the main section of gangline

- **Wheel dog** – dog(s) that run closest to the sled

- **Yukon Quest** – 1,000-mile dogsled race from Whitehorse to Fairbanks

Epilogue

September 14, 2011. The team and I had just finished a great training run on a crisp fall morning, and, dogs unharnessed and happily lounging, I headed to the house for a coffee. Hearing the door, Tanya came up from her office with a quizzical look on her face.

"What's up?" I asked.

"Well, I just had an interesting phone call. How badly do you want to find the funds to run Iditarod this winter?" she asked with a smirk. I started to grow concerned with the direction this conversation was headed. I raised an eyebrow, and Tanya continued. "A lady who followed the team during the Yukon Quest and is from a large company in Toronto just called. She wanted to know if you would come and speak to their executive team on how you train leaders, build teams, and deal with overcoming all the challenges that you face while travelling 1,000 miles through the wilderness. She feels what we do, the stories, and the lessons would be really relevant to what they do as leaders in their company and would be different from any speakers they have ever brought in before. I told her I didn't think you would be interested, but she also mentioned that they pay *really* well and that it would only be for an hour while they were having dinner. It is only their senior executive team, so would only be about 20 people."

I shook my head. "Nope, it doesn't matter what they are offering. I am not going to Toronto to stand on a stage and speak to a group of incredibly successful business people. I don't fit into that world!"

Tanya smirked. "I told her that was what you would say. She asked us to talk about it and call her back tomorrow."

"There is nothing to think about," I answered over my shoulder, heading to the kitchen.

That evening, Tanya brought it up again. She said, "You wouldn't have to do it alone, you know. We could share the stage and present together. I could build the bridges between their world and ours and compare, then you could share your stories to bring the principles alive. You could take your sled to share the tools that you need to do your job well and compare to the tools they need to do theirs. I think we could put together a really relevant presentation, and it might be fun. Plus, I bet they will never have had a musher speak to them before, and it would more than cover the Iditarod entry fee!" What she said made sense, but I still wasn't sold. I agreed to think on it.

The next morning, I had a moment of weakness, and when Tanya said she had to call the lady back and looked at me questioningly, I grumbled, "Fine, but just this one time!"

Tanya spent a pile of time the next month putting together and building a powerful PowerPoint presentation. It showcased images depicting everything from training to drop bags to the races themselves, put to music. We also spent time reverse engineering what we do to build a team, develop leaders (are they born or made?) and deal with the challenges that are thrown at us on the trail. Everything from weather to trail conditions, psychology, leadership, and team dynamics as we all work towards a huge goal and vision. The mindset it takes to travel 1,000 miles. We went back remembering the many stories we had working with the dogs over the years, picking out the ones that best represented the topics they wanted us to address.

Finally, the day arrived. We packed the sled with all the normal gear I would carry on a race, including my cold weather clothing, and, with our notes and computer in the truck, headed out on the 3-hour drive to Toronto. To say I was having second thoughts about this whole thing is a huge understatement. I grew more anxious the closer we got, and, as we neared Toronto, Tanya announced she was really nervous. Ha! She was the extrovert and the one with speaking experience. If she was nervous, how did she think I felt? She had been studying the outline and notes she had made for the speech for the last hour and looked up at one point and said, "But how do you keep going when things are bad?" I knew someone was going to ask that, and it is a good question. I thought for a bit, but I honestly wasn't sure how to put it into words.

"What goes through your mind when you hit a section that you are scared of?" Tanya asked.

Turning back is not possible, I replied. "In my mind, I convince myself turning back means we might not have enough supplies to get back to the last checkpoint. It means the checkpoint might be closed and there will be no one there to connect with you and Ward and we'll be stuck there. I go through all kinds of scenarios where turning around has way worse outcomes than moving ahead."

Tanya nodded. "That makes total sense and can apply to many situations," she murmured as she began writing in her notes again.

We pulled into the Toronto airport hotel where the meetings were being held, and, after being shown which part of the conference centre the group was in, we pulled up to the door and started unloading all our gear—when you unload a dogsled outside of a big hotel in a city you certainly draw attention! With Tanya carrying the front of the sled and me the back with all the gear packed in it, we made our way through the doors into the hotel. The afternoon meeting was still in session as we were a bit early, so we waited outside the room for them to come out. Both of us full of nerves by this point. I was wearing jeans, sneakers, a sweater, and ball cap. As the doors opened and the executives moved out into the hall, I felt totally out of place. Besides how we were dressed and the loaded dogsled with an axe and snowshoes sticking out of it sitting outside their meeting room, the questioning glances led us to believe they were not expecting us as their dinner keynote speakers. We glanced at each other; how the hell had I let Tanya talk me into this? My stomach was doing summersaults.

The lady who had hired us came up to us with a big smile and warm welcome. Tanya said, "I take it they didn't know we were coming?" She laughed good naturedly and said, "No, I kept it a surprise." She helped us get everything into the room and closed the doors while we set up. Everyone was really helpful with getting the PowerPoint and screen set up and audio and mics tested. Everything was in place, and dinner was ready to be served. Susan opened the doors, and the group came in and started taking their seats with many glances of open curiosity directed our way.

Our loaded sled outside the Marriott Hotel in Toronto
before the presentation

The doors closed, and all eyes moved to the stage. Susan glanced our way, and Tanya nodded, whispering in my ear, "I'm feeling a bit terrified right now…" She wasn't alone, being at the starting line of a 1,000-mile race doesn't feel this nerve wracking! Susan picked up the mic and started introducing us, telling her coworkers how she had heard about us from a supplier that had come into her office last February. Knowing she was a dog lover, he empathetically told her she had to follow this guy from Ontario as he and his huskies travelled across the Yukon and Alaska and that she could follow his GPS tracker at any point to see where he was. She admitted she got addicted to watching the tracker, to the point of making excuses of forgetting something in her office to run back and refresh the tracker to see where the team and I were. I had no idea…

With a warm round of welcoming applause, Susan turned the stage over to us. Tanya stepped up and started sharing our story of how we quit our jobs and our lives went to the dogs—literally. Laughter rang out from some of her stories. Then she cued the presentation, saying it would allow us to put them into our world better than our words could. The room went dark and, on a massive screen with speakers turned up loud, Tanya's PowerPoint started with a beautiful shot of Hosta in one of our playyards. It then moved to the team training, the Iditarod, and then the Yukon Quest, finishing with a picture of Lily and me. I had seen the presentation on her computer as she put it together, but seeing our dogs on that huge screen with the loud music surrounding us like in a movie theatre caught me off guard. As the presentation drew to an end, I glanced at Tanya and saw tears running down her face. I wasn't dry-eyed, either. Tanya motioned towards the crowd, and I saw some of the audience discreetly wiping their eyes. Our incredible dogs had worked their magic. Even though they weren't here with us in person, they were connecting with our audience.

As the PowerPoint ended, a loud round of applause started in the back corner and quickly filled the room. The lights came back on, and Tanya stepped to the centre of the stage. She shared some of her lessons on how we had learned to overcome setbacks, how they had been our greatest teacher, and how we built great teams. She nodded to me, and I moved the sled into position. She asked everyone to check under their coffee cups. Before they had come back into the room, she had put a slip of paper under 6 cups on various tables. She asked anyone who found a piece of paper to please come to the front of the room for a demonstration. She also asked the CEO to come up. Now we had everyone's attention! Tanya had written instructions on each slip of paper with a position on the team. She instructed the lead dogs to take their spot on the gangline, the team dogs to take their spot, and the wheel dogs to stand close to the sled. She then showed the CEO where he would stand as the musher of the team. She mentioned that all the "team members" should do the first instruction on the slip of paper when their musher asked them to move. Going back to the CEO, she told him to go ahead and get his team moving. He looked at her and then, standing on the runners said, "Uh, lets go!" One team member sat down, another went in circles, another went backwards, one howled, one pulled right, and one pulled left. It was pandemonium, and everyone was laughing hysterically. Tanya explained how for a dogteam— or any team—to move forward, they had to have a clear vision from their leader. That vision had to be communicated effectively to the entire team with specific directions on what each team member's role was. Everyone had to be on the same page and understand where they were headed. Tanya told the CEO the correct term to get a dogteam moving was "hike," along with a quick push of the sled to get it moving in the right direction. She asked the "team" to follow the second instruction on their sheet of paper, and with the CEO's "hike!" his team of six, along with his push in the right direction, had him and the sled easily moving across the carpeted floor of the conference room like he was on snow. Everyone laughed as they took their seats. Tanya went on to ask them how well they knew their own team members in each division. She talked about how we traveled with the dogs so much and spent so much time with them that I knew each dog incredibly well; what is their favourite position to run in, who they like working with best, who they like working with least, what conditions and situations they thrive in, what conditions and situations they get stressed or scared in. I knew by watching them run how they were feeling physically and emotionally and what it takes to adjust that. People were taking notes as they ate.

Tanya glanced my way and nodded. She started talking about me, saying really kind words about what I meant to her and finishing with, "He would rather be heading out into a blizzard or facing an angry moose than standing here about to speak, but his incredible stories are unlike what you will likely have ever heard before." She sure wasn't wrong. I would take -50°C and a storm any day over being about to have 25 sets of eyes on me waiting to hear me speak. Public speaking was one of my biggest fears.

As we had agreed, Tanya stayed on the stage with me. I always feel at home on my sled, so I was to start with telling them about my sled and the tools the dogs and I needed to travel that kind of distance in winter conditions. I felt like I was tripping over my words, I felt sick, this was a disaster. I held up my knife that was custom made for my hand in a little craftsman shop in Alaska—one of my most important and prized tools. I started talking about it and held it up for the crowd to see. The CEO, who was sitting at the front table right in front of me, stood up and held up his hand with his cell phone extended. He said, "I will trade you this blackberry for that knife!" At that time, that blackberry was the icon of all cell phones, and my reply was, "not a chance in hell!" The crowd erupted in laughter, and I chuckled. The ice was broken, and I was grateful to him for helping to put me a bit more at ease.

The rest of our hour with them went quickly as I shared stories from the Iditarod and Yukon Quest trail about our beloved dogs and how incredible they were. How my mindset as the leader is the single biggest factor in how the team will do. How what I am feeling without saying a word is felt by my dogs and how they respond accordingly to what I feel. How when you build a great team, as their leader, you have to, at times, put your trust in your team to get you through. For me, that is sometimes life and death, and my team doesn't let me down. However, trust is a two-way street, and they put their trust in me. I would never break that trust or let them down—if I did, that would be the end of our journey. You can't break trust; it is all for one and one for all. We also talked about the value of each team member, how the team could not possibly move forward without the right team members in each role. A team was only as great as their leader, but a leader only as great as their team.

As we finished, Tanya said, "If we could install the heart, the passion, and the drive into your organization that is in our huskies, there is nothing your company couldn't accomplish!"

A standing ovation followed. We were blown away and incredibly humbled. Questions started flying, and for the next 30 minutes, we shared more stories. When that ended, people lined up to come talk to us and ask us more questions and share how our presentation resonated with them. When the last audience member had left, Susan came up and, smiling, said that went so well. "I'm going to have you come back in a month and give the same presentation to another part of our organization. So much for my "We'll do this once!"

After our second presentation, Susan kindly sent us this testimonial from her executive team:

"I had the honour of having Tanya and Hank speak at our management meeting on September 21, 2011. The feedback that I received was unprecedented: our team was overwhelmingly positive about the presentation; everyone found it interesting and were able to see the clear linkages between what we do as leaders in times of challenge and that of Hank assessing and developing his leaders, creating a team that can work in alignment, and then through a relationship of trust, leading that team 1,000 miles across Alaska and the Yukon. Hank and Tanya's easy and down-to-earth style really resonated with our audience. I will be having them back to deliver the same presentation to another group of our leadership team in November. The following quotes round out the sentiments of some of the audience members: "Fantastic, very genuine and from the heart. Directly applies to what we have learned [about leadership]. We should use them in other meetings". "Genuine, passionate presenters who were able to relate their business to our corporate environment". "Excellent presentation – Hank's charm was that he was 'real' and had the direct experience". "The content is excellent – Hank is accessing a very visceral part of the human experience and there is no such thing as a boring story or one that takes 'too long'; we love hearing about it. Tanya, you are a great natural presenter and the parallels you draw to corporate life are very pertinent. You and your team have a winning formula and boardrooms everywhere will benefit from your presentation".

Since then, we have had the honour of speaking for that company six times in Toronto and once in Vancouver (we had to use a luggage cart for the exercise instead of a sled in this one) to share the same presentation with their management teams there. While public speaking will never be my favourite thing to do, I do enjoy seeing how people connect with the stories and personalities of our dogs and will come up afterwards and say they think they are a leader like Lily, or they are the Jay on the team. I don't think Tanya or I have ever gotten through a presentation without each of us getting emotional sharing various stories. We watch our audience share laughter and tears during the presentations with us. Dogs have a way of breaking down people's walls, and, as an employee who had heard our presentation two times told the Vancouver team when he introduced us, "You are going to hear and learn about dogs—and yet I have never learned so much about people in a presentation before."

You truly never know where the trail is going to lead you…

Not Ready For The Journey To End?

Check out how you can jump on a virtual or real dogsled and stay on the trail with our huskies and family year around.

Our Virtual Dogsled Tours

Literally feel like you are on the runners with Hank as he heads out with some of our huskies on an adventure through the wilderness. We have several different virtual tours available from an introductory tour where Dustyn will teach you how to dogsled and Michaela & Jessica will introduce you to the huskies on your team to running a team of 6 in early winter. There is a run with some of the veteran raceteam that are featured in this book, even at 13 they know they are special!! Or go on a powerful run with the Avengers, our new up and coming raceteam. These tours are fabulously fun and have received glowing reviews for families, schools and retirement residences. vtour.winterdance.com

Join us in person!

Hop on the runners of a dogsled yourself! Every winter we have the absolute privilege of welcoming guests from around the Globe to meet our beloved huskies and travel through our 2000 acres of wilderness with our family.

Learn more and book a tour on **www.winterdance.com**. You will also find a video on our homepage about our kennel, our huskies and this crazy lifestyle we adore.

Keep up to date on all things Winterdance by popping into our world daily via the magic of social media. During fall and winter don't miss our live fireside chats each week.

 www.facebook.com/winterdancedogsledtours/
 www.instagram.com/winterdancedogsledtours

Our Biggest Life Lessons Have Come From Our Huskies

Join us for a FREE video series

In this 10-part mini-series, we will share with you, life changing lessons that our huskies have taught us as well as amazing stories from the trail. Lessons that have allowed us and our huskies to finish 1000-mile races, build the business, family and lifestyle that we had dreamed of. These are the same lessons that we share with senior management teams of major corporations. Visit **videos.winterdance.com**.

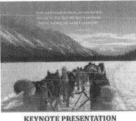

Looking for a Unique Presentation for your Team?

We share our principles on building incredible teams, leading through challenging times, finding your vision and how a leader's mindset is the most vital piece of all., We include stories that will leave your audience on the edge of their seats, laughing or possibly crying. Our presentation is delivered from the heart and is about our incredible dogs, but their stories will leave your team with a whole new perspective on how to lead and work together to accomplish all of their goals.

For more information contact: **info@winterdance.com**

Catch the next book in the series of the team's adventure coming in 2021

With the decision to sign up for Iditarod behind us, my next big decision was going to be Lily. At almost 11 years of age, she didn't look older than 8, but she was turning 11. I shouldn't even be considering her to be on the raceteam this winter…should I? Strider would not be on the team this year. He'd just pushed himself too hard, and at 11 as well, I wasn't going to risk him doing that again. Losing his amazing skills and the deep bond and trust I have with him would be hard enough; could I leave Lily behind, too, and the leadership I needed at the front of this team when things got tough as they inevitably would? Maverick's leadership skills were coming along nicely, but he was still a 3-year-old, and maturity and experience are so important in a great distance lead dog.

With September's first cool night (8°C), it was time to start training. Lily was screaming to go as I pulled out the harnesses and drove the ATV in the yard. I decided to let her start training with the team and see how she did. At the first hint it was too much for her, my decision would be made and she would retire from the raceteam. The guides would love having her join them for tours, as would our guests!

Lily thrived on her first run, second run, and then all the runs that fall. No one would ever guess she was almost 11 years old. I found myself wishing I didn't know she was. She commanded leadership in the team, as she always had, giving the youngsters (who were her children and grandchildren) a glare if she didn't approve of what they were or were not doing, even going so far occasionally as swinging back hard, under full run, to nip someone who was not doing their job well enough, in her opinion. Lily runs a tight ship; she would not be most people's idea of a fun boss!

Lily and Maverick lead a fall training run

By December, she was not only keeping up with the team but possibly doing better than she ever had before. While in September I had let her start training to put off a hard decision for a bit, I had not really expected to be seriously considering taking her to Alaska. As the team went over 1,000 miles in training, I found my mind thinking "what if?" during training runs. What if I can take her? She clearly wants to run and is doing amazing, imagine having Lily at the front of the team leading us to Nome this winter…

January saw us headed to Michigan for the Seney 300. This would give me a good idea of whether it would be too much for her in a low stress race. We all *loved* the Seney! The trails, the people, it is just an amazing time, and since most of the team had run there now three times, they were as comfortable going back there as Ward and I were.

Lily was at the head of the team, screaming and howling to hit the trail as we hooked the team up for the start. At the end of day 1, she looked as good as all the younger dogs. The end of day 2 found her still in lead and in her element. Day 3 as we crossed the finish line saw no change. The veterinarians at the Seney, who I highly respect, had been watching her extra close during the race at my request. Dr. Tom came up to me at the finish and said, "Hank, she looks amazing. You would never guess her age. There have been 11 and even a couple of 12-year-old dogs run the Iditarod."

Another month of training runs on our home trails didn't help, either. Lily was still doing great. A week before we were set to load up and head for Alaska, all the raceteam had an appointment with our Dr. Laurie. She would do full physicals on each dog, Bordetella injections, and make sure all their microchips were findable and then sign off on Iditarod paperwork for the dogs' health. This was my last opportunity to have someone tell me Lily should stay in Haliburton. Laurie knew well my battle over Lily and spent twice as much time on her physical as everyone else's. With her work done, she looked at me and said, "I know you want me to tell you she can't go, but I can't. This dog is physiologically no older than an 8-year-old dog. She is incredible." Damn! Now the decision was completely mine.

We trained every day over the next week, and I watched Lily like a hawk, looking for any sign at all that she didn't want to go with us or couldn't. I saw nothing, not the slightest limp, not a hint of hesitation in her that she was trying too hard to keep up with the younger dogs, no sign at all that she wanted to be anywhere else other than exactly where she was—leading the most amazing dog team I have ever had and ready to head to Alaska.

February 20, everything was packed and loaded in the truck, checked and double-checked. All that was left was to load the dogs and drive down our driveway. I looked at Tanya and said, "What do you think?" She answered, "Laurie gave you no reason Lily couldn't go, Lily has given you no reason she can't go, she wants to go and you know how badly you want her at the front of that team, and so do I. She will take care of all of you." My decision was made. Lily would go to Alaska with us. We were taking two extra dogs so if something changed between here and the start line, I still had the option to not take her.

The dogs were let out of the kennel and ripped through the yard around the truck. They always know the difference between a normal truck ride for a training run and a big trip! They even seem to know the difference between shorter drives to races compared with heading to Alaska. This was a big deal. Lily exploded out of the kennel like the rest of the team and was jumping up on me like everyone else to get on the truck. She, better than any of them, knew where we were headed, and she wanted to go. If I was honest with myself, I couldn't have been happier.

Four days later, we stopped for a training run in Whitehorse on the way to Anchorage. Lily was a bit stiffer than the younger dogs but shook it off quickly and was running beautifully with the team. Her grandson Maverick was in lead beside her, as he was on a lot of our runs. Not every dog can/will run beside Lily, but Maverick's easygoing personality was a good fit for hers.

We rolled into Anchorage on Wednesday, three days before the ceremonial start, four days before the official start. So much had to be done; from more vet checks, meeting after meeting, final packing and shopping for anything we had forgotten or still needed, the banquet, and hopefully 2-3 training runs still. The boys were super excited to be back in Alaska, and the dogs were, too. Moose were *everywhere*! The snow was so deep this winter that they were all along the road and by houses so they could move easier and not be such easy prey to wolves.

We did a training run, and all the dogs looked great. Vet checks at Iditarod include blood work and EKGs on every dog. This was my last chance to have a verified reason that Lily couldn't run. When the results came back, though, yet again, there was no evidence that she was turning 11 years old and should stay back. Tanya, Barb, and the girls arrived in Anchorage just in time for the banquet, and after that big production, we sat down to make the final decision of the team. Tanya was coming for a training run with me tomorrow, and we would watch Lily for any signs to help us decide.

Of course, that training run was one of those perfect runs. The dogs were all happy and ran smoothly, attitudes were all high, excitement was higher, and Lily was leading the fray.

Saturday's ceremonial start was a 12-mile run through the streets of Anchorage to the military base for sponsors, race fans, and media. It didn't count, and, as such, the dogs that ran the ceremonial start (only 12) did not have to be the dogs on your team at the official start the next day. Lily and Maverick were harnessed and put in lead for this run. Lily would take us anywhere, and nothing really phased Maverick as far as big crowds, noise, or running through towns. Logan drove the second sled, and our IditaRider was a lot of fun. Everything about that 12-mile run was fun, from the fans singing "Oh Canada" as we passed to being handed more food than we could possibly eat—from home-baked treats to BBQ hotdogs and burgers to even beer. Alaskan hospitality at its finest! Even a Canadian flag was hung off a tree to celebrate us Canucks in the race. We pulled into the runway of the military base and the finish line of the ceremonial start with all tails flagging high and spirits equally high, looking for Tanya, Ward, and our truck.

We unsnapped the dogs from the gangline and put them out around the truck for a good warm soup that Ward and Tanya had waiting with the other five dogs already out waiting for us. I took extra time unharnessing Lily, carefully moving each joint and watching for any sign of soreness—nothing. Like everyone else, Lily wolfed down her soup.

Dogs happy from their run and with a full stomach, they were settled into their beds on the truck as we headed back to the Millenium Hotel where we were staying. The sled all had to be packed in preparation for tomorrow's official start, and no matter how prepared you felt, there was always last-minute things needed. The rest of the day passed quickly, and as bed time neared, we went out to care for the dogs again before they would settle in for a good night's sleep, as I also hoped to do. I sat and talked to Lily, silly I know, hoping for an answer from those steel blue eyes. I got nothing.

As we headed to bed, Tanya asked me if I had decided about Lily. I shook my head. My last night for a good sleep for over a week was wasted. I tossed and turned all night with nerves for the start tomorrow, but as Tanya woke and turned to me around 4 a.m., she looked at me and said, "Are you sleeping at all?" I replied, "Not really." She said, "Lily?" I nodded. Dawn broke, it was time to get moving. I felt ill. This was my third 1,000-mile race, you would think I would get used to the nerves, but apparently, I hadn't yet. Breakfast for me wasn't an option.

Dogs fed, sled all packed and loaded in the truck, it was time to head to the start. I still had no idea whether Lily was going or not, and it weighed heavy on my mind—and everything that could possibly go wrong for the next 1,000 miles. Ward, Tanya, and I arrived at the official start in Wasilla about an hour north of Anchorage. The kids would come with Barb closer to the start. The next two hours would fly by. Dogs off the truck for a stretch, drink, and snack and to watch all the activity as we pulled the sled off and for the sixth time, I went through it to make sure we had everything we would need and all the required gear; headlamp ready with new batteries, harnesses out, gangline stretched out ready for the hookup, snow hooks sunk, and the sled tethered off to the truck. My race bib lay on top of the sledbag waiting. Veterinarians came along to check all the dogs and make sure all had Iditarod ID tags and their microchips were working. Then, with the excitement rising by the minute and the crowds growing, the dogs went back on the truck to rest for a bit. No sense getting them all worked up too soon before the start.

The kids and Barb arrived; it was almost time to start getting ready. I put on my big suit and heavy boots, put my headlamp on so it would be ready when dusk came, and started some handwarmers in my big outer mitts so they would be warm when I needed them. One by one, the dogs came off the truck to start getting their harnesses on. Tanya looked at me as I approached Lily's spot on the truck. I looked at her with the question in my eyes. She nodded and said, "Take her. If you send her back after a couple hundred miles, that would be fine, too, if she wants to go. Glory knows you want to take her and have her brilliance out there with you, and I want you to have her out there looking out for all of you." I opened Lily's door. She always hopped right into my arms, but this time, she didn't move. She looked at me and stayed at the back of her bed. I said "Lil?" She didn't move. I asked again, and she stared at me. She wasn't coming out. She had decided for me. She wouldn't be going with me to Nome, not this time. I reached in and rubbed her head, staring her in the eyes and felt so emotional leaving her behind. Could we do this without her? I closed her door. I also worried she was ok. Tanya assured me she would have a vet check her as soon as she got back to the truck.

We quickly harnessed all the dogs, with the boys helping and the girls being given the job of trying to keep Zeus, Jester, Viper, Charlie, and Scully from loosing their minds in their eagerness to follow the other teams and get going. Dogs all on the gangline and 12 volunteers in place, Ward took his spot at the front of the team, leading Maverick and Scully. Tanya hopped on the sled runners beside me, riding the break as I pulled the snowhooks and gave each of the kids a hug and pulled the knot loose in the line holding the sled to the truck. We lunged forward until the handlers put pressure with the leashes on the gangline, slowing the dogs down. We moved to the first stop sign. With Ward's hand up, all Tanya's and my weight on the brake, and the handlers pulling back with all their might, we stopped the team. Sixteen crazed, muscled huskies are an insane amount of power. Every two minutes, as another team left the starting chute, we would move forward to the next stop sign.

Finally, we were next, and we pulled under the starting sign. I quickly sunk both snowhooks and handed the brake and sled off to volunteers, with other volunteers stepping up beside the sled to hold it in place. The kids were all there, and I ran up to the front of the team, petting and talking to each dog as we waited the two-minute count down. They could see the team in front of us going across the lake, and they wanted to follow and just run so badly. The noise was deafening, and crowds lined both sides of the snowfences along the course all the way across the lake. We hit the 30-second announcement. I went and hugged each of the kids again. Jessica was in Tanya's arms, and I hugged both of them with an "I love you" and Tanya's "I love you, please be safe, see you in Nome!"

I ran to the sled, and she ran to the front of the team, still carrying Jessica. The volunteers on my brake stepped away, and as the countdown hit 10, Tanya waved the handlers away from the dogs. Ward stepped back, and, as I reached down to pull my snowhooks, my hands were shaking so hard I could hardly pull them. I was about to unleash 800 lbs. of insanity, and there was no way I would be able to control them for at least 10 miles until the madness to run had eased a bit. I was just the guy on the back of the sled.

Three…two…one…go! We were off. I high-fived Tanya on the way by and we sprinted across the lake in deep, churned-up snow. My thoughts turned to Lily. I hoped she was ok. God knows I would miss her guiding this team deeply.

I wouldn't know for several days until Tanya flew into McGrath to see me that when they all got back to the truck and let the dogs out while they packed up, she went to Lily's box and opened it and Lily jumped right out and was bouncing around like a puppy. Tanya said she wished she had a way to let me know that Lily was fine and that several hours later she was flaked out on the hotel bed with the kids watching cartoons, and that she quite enjoyed the life of leisure for the next two weeks while the team and I journeyed to Nome. She had done her job; she had trained all of us hard that winter and gotten us to the starting line. She knew where she was and decided she wasn't going to Nome; it was up to us now to finish this journey she had started with us.

Lily enjoying hotel life and cartoons with Logan & Michaela

About Defining Moments Press

Built for aspiring authors who are looking to share transformative ideas with others throughout the world, Defining Moments Press offers life coaches, healers, business professionals, and other non-fiction or self-help authors a comprehensive solution to get their book published without breaking the bank or taking years.

Defining Moments Press prides itself on bringing readers and authors together to find tools and solutions for everyday problems.

As an alternative to self-publishing or signing with a major publishing housela we offer full profits to our authors, low-priced author copies, and simple contract terms.

Most authors get stuck trying to navigate the technical end of publishing. The comprehensive publishing services offered by Defining Moments Press mean that your book will be designed by an experienced graphic artist, available in printed, hard copy format, and coded for all eBook readers, including the Kindle, iPad, Nook, and more.

We handle all of the technical aspects of your book creation so you can spend more time focusing on your business that makes a difference for other people.

Defining Moments Press founder, publisher, and #1 bestselling author Melanie Warner has over 20 years of experience as a writer, publisher, master life coach, and accomplished entrepreneur.

You can learn more about Warner's innovative approach to self-publishing or take advantage of free trainings and education at: MyDefiningMoments.com

Defining Moments Book Publishing

If you're like many authors, you have wanted to write a book for a long time, maybe you have even started a book...but somehow, as hard as you have tried to make your book a priority, other things keep getting in the way.

Some authors have fears about their ability to write or whether or not anyone will value what they write or buy their book. For others, the challenge is making the time to write their book or having accountability to finish it.

It's not just finding the time and confidence to write that is an obstacle. Most authors get overwhelmed with the logistics of finding an editor, finding a support team, hiring an experienced designer, and figuring out all the technicalities of writing, publishing, marketing, and launching a book. Others have actually written a book and might have even published it but did not find a way to make it profitable.

For more information on how to participate in our next Defining Moments Author Training program, visit: www.MyDefiningMoments.com. Or you can email melanie@MyDefiningMoments.com.

Other Books by Defining Moments™ Press

- *Defining Moments: Coping With the Loss of a Child* - by Melanie Warner

- *Write your Bestselling Book in 8 Weeks or Less and Make a Profit - Even if No One Has Ever Heard of You* - by Melanie Warner

- *Become Brilliant: Roadmap From Fear to Courage* — by Shiran Cohen

- *Rise, Fight, Love, Repeat: Ignite Your Morning Fire* - by Jeff Wickersham

- *Life Mapping: Decoding the Blueprint of Your Soul* - by Karen Loenser

- *Ravens and Rainbows: A Mother-Daughter Story of Grit, Courage and Love After Death* — by L. Grey and Vanessa Lynn

- *Pivot You! 6 Powerful Steps to Thriving During Uncertain Times* — by Suzanne R. Sibilla

- *A Workforce Inspired: Tools to Manage Negativity and Support a Toxic-Free Workplace* — by Dolores Neira

- *Bouncing Back From Divorce With Vitality and Purpose*: A Strategy for Dads — by Nigel J Smart, PHD

- *Emerging You: A New Path A New Path to Leaving the Past Behind, Finding Your Purpose, and Becoming the Best Version of You* — by Soodabeh Mokry, RN, CHt

Made in the USA
Columbia, SC
24 September 2021